St Cuthbert's Corpse

A Life After Death

— DAVID WILLEM —

Sacristy Press
PO Box 612, Durham, DH1 9HT

www.sacristy.co.uk

Published in 2013 by Sacristy Press, Durham

Sacristy Limited, registered in England & Wales, number 7565667

British Library Cataloguing-in-Publication Data
A catalogue record for the book is available from the British Library

ISBN 978-1-908381-15-6

For Z, R & F

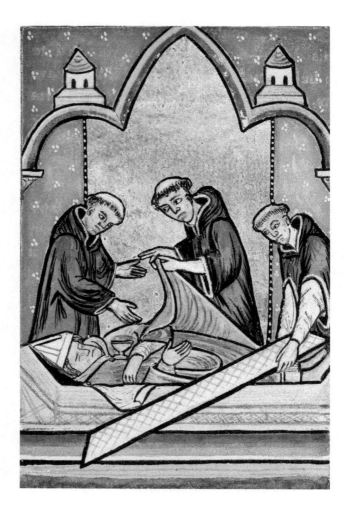

▲ *A nineteenth-century copy of a twelfth-century miniature illustration from the illuminated manuscript of The Life of St Cuthbert showing monks opening his coffin in 698, eleven years after his death, and finding his body incorrupt. Cuthbert is depicted not as a monk but as a twelfth-century bishop. Durham Cathedral Library Additional Manuscript 149, p. 38, (1828). Copyright the Chapter of Durham Cathedral.*

Preface

This started life as a travel book. Like many people who know Durham, I was aware of the story of the founding of the city: how the monks fled Lindisfarne after being attacked by Vikings; how they took with them a coffin containing the miraculously incorrupt corpse of their former bishop, St Cuthbert; and how, as they passed the still-forested site that would become Durham, the cart with the coffin on it got stuck fast in the mire. It would only move when they took the decision to follow a milkmaid and her lost cow towards "Dunholme"—the monks took this as a sign from St Cuthbert that he wanted his corpse to rest there.

I knew there was a record of this journey from Lindisfarne to Durham, and I thought it might be interesting to follow the route, comparing the world of the beginning of the third millennium with the end of the first. But, as I researched the possibility, I began to realise that there was hardly any detail to compare and that the actual route the monks took was more or less conjectural. At the same time, I started to realise that there was a second, much bigger story obscuring the first: the journey of the corpse through time.

It was in AD 698, eleven years after Cuthbert's death, that the monks first discovered that his body had not rotted—a miracle that was recorded by Bede, the first historian of the English people. But it intrigued me to learn that this was not the only time that the corpse was examined. On five other occasions, over 1,200 years, the possessors of the corpse took it upon themselves to open the coffin. It happened around 934, after the Viking invasion, in order to mark the resurgence of the Anglo-Saxon kings; it happened in 1104, following the Norman conquest; it happened in 1539, during the dissolution of the monasteries; it happened in 1827, as a part of the Protestant enlightenment; and it happened most recently in 1899, at the dawning of our own democratic, scientific age. This is a list that reads like the chapters in a child's history book from the middle of the twentieth century.

It was almost as if, every few generations, as the axis of the political, religious or intellectual world shifted around them, the people who possessed the corpse felt a compulsion to revisit it—to examine it, to associate themselves with its power, and to affirm what remained. And, on almost every occasion the body was disturbed, someone kept a record. Sometimes there are two.

This quickly became the subject of the book. I was excited to lay before the people of the north east, and all those who love Durham, a new perspective on the history of the city and the Cathedral: how both were founded on the miracle of an incorrupt corpse and how the condition of that corpse continued to matter, right into modern times. I soon realised it was also an opportunity to bring together all the accounts of the openings of the coffin into a single volume for the first time.

Beyond this, I have added almost nothing.

Acknowledgements

It was a challenge to come to some understanding of all the material that is available, and it was hard work trying to marshal it all into a coherent narrative. But, as much of the material is not my own, I need to thank many people I have never met, while making it very clear that they bear no responsibility for what follows.

First, I need to thank the late C.F. Battiscombe, a man whose given names I do not even know, but whose monumental, completist *Relics of Saint Cuthbert* is a volume so substantial that it can only be carried to and from Durham's Clayport Library in a bag-for-life, or a hod. And I have had it on loan on and off for most of the last three years.

Then I need to thank Professor David Rollason. I have read quite a bit of his work, and this has made me so aware of his focused, concentrated intelligence that, despite his being very much alive, I have found it easier not to meet him. I just know that if I did, his fierce, forensic brilliance would reveal the chasms of my vast ignorance of, well, everything he has dedicated his life to. All I can say is that I have enjoyed filling the very, very bottom of some of those chasms with a tiny bit of his scholarship.

Then there are the people whom I haven't met whose work has influenced perhaps only a few sentences in this book, but who nevertheless revolutionised my understanding of what was sayable. They are Dr Elizabeth Coatsworth for her essay on Cuthbert's golden-garnet cross, and Professor Richard Bailey for his research into the nineteenth-century openings of Cuthbert's grave (both of which can be found in Bonner, Rollason and Stancliffe's *Saint Cuthbert, His Cult and His Community*). I also need to thank the late Geoffrey Moorhouse, whose *The Last Office* helped me understand how the dissolution of the monasteries played itself out in Durham. Finally, in the unmet category, I need to thank Dr Sam Lucy for saying something on the phone that made a huge difference: that three of the other four pectoral crosses that have been found were associated with women.

Then there are the people I have had the nerve to meet and who were much more generous with their thoughts and contacts than I had any right to expect. They were Roger Norris, the former Chapter Librarian at the Cathedral, who helped me scope out the project; Gabriel Sewell, Head of Collections at the Cathedral, who found me a piece of the original Anglo-Saxon coffin to examine (it looks, by the way, like chocolate brownie and smells of old, damp spices); Lilian Groves, the chief guide at the Cathedral, and Seif El Rashidi, coordinator of Durham World Heritage Site, for talking me though everything I couldn't understand; and Dr Giles Gasper for suggesting I contact the publishers and for reading some of the manuscript. I also spent a happy hour with Professor Richard Gameson trying to persuade him that the strap line for the 2013 Lindisfarne Gospels exhibition in Durham should be something like *The Book that Made England*. I imagine his hour was more frustrating, but he was both charming and incisive in his rebuttal, and I can only say I hope he has forgiven me.

I also want to ask forgiveness of some important dead people. I have spent the last couple of years in the company of the few people who may have actually seen Cuthbert's corpse: Fowler, Brown, Kitchin, Raine, Bates, Reginald, Symeon and a couple of anonymous monks. Because my mind has been bending on the same material, I have become attuned to their nuances and little evasions and they have ended up feeling to me a bit like family members—dead ones. So I want to be forgiven, both for this presumption, and for the liberties I have taken re-paragraphing much of their writing. I even re-paragraphed Bede. I certainly would not like it if he re-paragraphed me.

And then of course there is Cuthbert himself. I don't feel at all like I know him. He is mysterious: like Hamlet's father's ghost, a tall, stern, irascible, contradictory figure, who was nevertheless quite attractive to women. I am not sure how far I should have gone with this aspect of his life. I could have gone further, but then I may already have gone too far. However, I have been intrigued by the friendship that Cuthbert had with Princess Aelfflaed. This may only be because this is such a male story—monk, hermit, priest, heroic cadaver—that the appearance of Aelfflaed, a royal abbess and Anglo-Saxon power broker, introduces both a female perspective and the intrigue of a relationship between a man and a woman into what would otherwise be an exclusively masculine narrative. The fact is she knowingly represented the temptations of the world, and, although the relationship between Cuthbert and Aelfflaed can only be glimpsed through the accounts of religious men, there seems to be something there. Apologies to both of them if I have got the wrong end of the stick.

David Willem
May 2013

Contents

CHAPTER ONE

The Death of Cuthbert

20 March 687

He was in his mid-fifties and sick, aware that he was dying. Yet, on the day after Christmas in the year AD 686, the man whose corpse would one day have such power chose to leave his monastery on Lindisfarne to go, once again, to live alone on a stud of rock in the North Sea.

His fellow monks went with him to the Lindisfarne shore. The oldest of them, another sick man, asked the question on everybody's mind.

"Tell us, my Lord Bishop, when we may hope for your return?"

"When you shall bring my body back here," he replied.[1]

He was going to spend the vicious winter alone on an island called Inner Farne. His only shelter against the storms was a mud-walled, straw-roofed hovel; scratched into the ground, his latrine, a hut balanced on two pieces of driftwood wedged across a fissure in the rocks. During the few years he had previously lived as a hermit on the island, he had banked a circle of earth and stone around both his dwelling and his oratory—the hut he used for prayer. It stopped him seeing over to the mainland, preventing his mind from straying. All he could do was look up to the sun, the stars and the clouds, and the birds—the endless, wheeling universe of birds in their hopeless planetarium.

"He shut himself up in his cell away from the sight of men," wrote Bede, who found out about his life from the monks who knew him, "and spent his time alone in fasting, watching, and prayer, rarely having communication with any one without, and that through the

1

window, which at first was left open, that he might see and be seen; but, after a time, he shut that also, and opened it only to give his blessing, or for any other purpose of absolute necessity."

Eight weeks after Christmas, in February 687, he suffered the first attack of what would be his final illness. And there is a record. A monk called Herefrith told Bede what happened.

For he was taken ill on the fourth day of the week; and again on the fourth day of the week his pains were over, and he departed to the Lord. But when I came to him on the first morning after his illness began (for I had also arrived at the island with the brethren three days before) in my desire to obtain his blessing and advice as usual, I gave the customary signal of my coming, and he came to the window, and replied to my salutation with a sigh.

"My Lord Bishop," said I, "what is the matter with you? Has your indisposition come upon you this last night?"

"Yes," said he, "indisposition has come upon me."

I thought that he was speaking of an old complaint, which vexed him almost every day, and not of a new malady; so, without making any more inquiries, I said to him, "Give us your blessing, for it is time to put to sea and return home."

"Do so," replied he; "go on board and return home in safety. But, when the Lord shall have taken my spirit, bury me in this house, near my oratory, towards the south, over against the eastern side of the holy cross, which I have erected there. Towards the north side of that same oratory is a sarcophagus covered with turf, which the venerable Abbot Cudda formerly gave me. You will place my body therein, wrapping it in linen, which you will find in it. I would not wear it whilst I was alive, but for the love of that highly favoured woman, who sent it to me, the Abbess Verca. I have preserved it to wrap my corpse in."

On hearing these words, I replied, "I beseech you, father, as you are weak, and talk of the probability of your dying, to let some of the brethren remain here to wait on you."

"Go home now," said he; "but return at the proper time."

So I was unable to prevail upon him, notwithstanding the urgency of my entreaties; and at last I asked him when we should return to him.

"When God so wills it," said he, "and when he himself shall direct you."

We did as he commanded us; and having assembled the brethren immediately in the church, I had prayers offered up for him without intermission; for, said I, it seems to me, from some words which he spoke, that the day is approaching on which he will depart to the Lord.

Herefrith was anxious to return to the island but was prevented by a storm that raged for five days.

At length there was a calm, and we went to the island, and found him away from his cell in the house where we were accustomed to reside. The brethren who came with me had some occasion to go back to the neighbouring shore, so that I was left alone on the island to minister to the holy father. I warmed some water and washed his feet, which had an ulcer from a long swelling; and from the quantity of blood that came from it, required to be attended to. I also warmed some wine which I had brought, and begged him to taste it: for I saw by his face that he was worn out with pain and want of food. When I had finished my service, he sat down quietly on the couch, and I sat down by his side.

Seeing that he kept silence, I said, "I see, my Lord Bishop, that you have suffered much from your complaint since we left you, and I marvel that you were so unwilling for us, when we departed, to send you some of our number to wait upon you."

He replied, "It was done by the providence and the will of God, that I might be left without any society or aid of man, and suffer somewhat of affliction. For when you were gone, my languor began to increase, so that I left my cell and came hither to meet any one who might be on his way to see me, that he might not have the trouble of going further. Now, from the moment of my coming until the present time, during a space of five days and five nights, I have sat here without moving."

"And how have you supported life, my Lord Bishop?" asked I; "have you remained so long without taking food?"

Upon which, turning up the couch on which he was sitting, he showed me five onions concealed therein, saying, "This has been my food for five days—for, whenever my mouth became too dry and parched with thirst, I cooled and refreshed myself by tasting these"; now one of the onions appeared to have been a little gnawed, but certainly not more than half of it was eaten; "and," continued he, "my enemies have never persecuted me so much during my whole stay in the island, as they have done during these last five days."

I was not bold enough to ask what kinds of persecutions he had suffered.

Herefrith did not leave him alone again. It was enough that Cuthbert, in unmedicated pain, had dragged himself to the hut near the landing place to wait for human comfort, and, this time, he was easily persuaded to allow some brothers to remain on the island to care for him. In the meantime, Herefrith rushed back to the monastery on Lindisfarne to talk to the other monks about what would happen to the body after Cuthbert died. For this was this question that now occupied the mind of the community.

Perhaps the sequence of events described by Bede has become confused, but Cuthbert's wishes are unclear. Despite his response to the question put to him on the Lindisfarne shore—i.e. that his body should return there after he was dead—at some point his intention was to be buried on Inner Farne. He wanted to be near to the oratory, in the sarcophagus given to him by Abbot Cudda and wrapped in the cloth given to him by Abbess Verca. He knows that after he is dead, "fugitives and criminals" will flee to his body, and that if he were to be buried back on Lindisfarne, its presence would become a burden. The community would then find it "necessary to intercede for such [men] before the secular rulers, and so you may have trouble on my account."

For the monastery however, what mattered more was that they controlled access to the corpse and its power—something much more easily done if it rested in the church on Lindisfarne rather than out on uninhabited, isolated Inner Farne. Herefrith therefore returned with a delegation to persuade Cuthbert, and, eventually, Cuthbert relented.

"Since you wish to overcome my scruples," he says, "and to carry my body amongst you, it seems to me to be the best plan to bury it in the inmost parts of the church, that you may be able to visit my tomb yourselves, and to control the visits of all other persons."

For the powers of the world were watching and the fate of Cuthbert's corpse mattered. On a hill on the mainland, almost opposite Inner Farne and commanding the short sea-route to Lindisfarne, is the fortress of Bamburgh, the citadel of the Northumbrian kings. Had the court been there, it would have watched as the drama of death and concern was played out. The royal family would have seen Cuthbert's boat leave Lindisfarne just after Christmas; seen his fire at night, the smoke during the day. They would have seen Herefrith and his fellow monks rowing back and forth, and shaken their heads at Cuthbert's isolation during the five days of winter storm. They would have heard the story—"Tell us, my Lord Bishop, when we may hope for your return?"—and his heroic reply.

For Cuthbert was much more to the court than an anchorite, much more than a curiosity on a hermitage just out to sea. He was also the Northumbrian royal family's chosen bishop and their court

soothsayer, a kind of Christian Merlin to these Anglo-Saxon Arthurs.
Perhaps he was even *of* the court himself. And, just as his choice of
resting place fell between between a lonely grave on Inner Farne and
a public tomb in the church of Lindisfarne, so too the whole of his
life had been stretched out between the periphery and the centre.
Ever since he had been a young squire, when he had ridden up to
the gate of the monastery at Melrose to ask about taking religious
vows, he had tried to escape to the edge of the world.

It was not that he had chosen not to live. He had always taken his
faith to the peasant people in the Northumbrian hills and showed
them how the power of this new, foreign religion could sometimes
cure their loved ones. He had consorted with kings and queens, and
he had found his way through the great religious controversy of his
times—the difference between the Celtic and Roman traditions
of Christianity in the land that was yet to become England. Yet,
at each stage of his life, he had tried to withdraw. From Melrose,
he had gone to the monastery on Lindisfarne which, then as now,
was cut off from the mainland twice a day by the tide. While on
Lindisfarne, he had gone to live as a hermit on one of the islets that
was only accessible at low tide, and finally, he had tried to live alone
out on Inner Farne.

But the more he retreated, the more spiritual authority was created
by his rejection of comfort, company, human love and human passion,
and the more this drew the world to him. Eventually it overwhelmed
him. One day, in the year 684, the king and the court determined
that he serve as bishop, if only for a couple of years.

It was a woman who brokered the deal. Her name was Aelfflaed.

She was a princess of the Northumbrian royal family and a
nun. In gratitude for a victory in battle, her father the late king had
dedicated her to chastity and the religious life, and Aelfflaed had
risen to become Abbess of Whitby.

She was thirty years old when the meeting took place; Cuthbert
was fifty. She summoned Cuthbert from Inner Farne to another

island, another piece of marginal land, this time in the mouth of the River Coquet on the sea route between Inner Farne and Whitby. Ostensibly, she had called him there because she wanted to see into the future.

She wanted to know when her brother Ecgfrid, the reigning king, would die. "For I know," she said, "that you abound in the spirit of prophecy, and that, if you are willing, you are able to tell me even this."

His reply seemed to predict that the king could be dead within a year.

The prophecy made her weep. But, "having wiped her face," Bede wrote, "she with feminine boldness adjured him by the majesty of the Holy One, that he would tell her who would be the heir to the kingdom, seeing that Ecgfrid had neither sons nor brothers."

Cuthbert thought for a moment. Then he reassured her that, despite the lack of heirs, the new king would be someone she could embrace with as much sisterly affection as she did the current king.

She pleaded with him to tell her where the heir might be found.

Again, Cuthbert was vague. "You behold this great and spacious sea", he said, "how it aboundeth in islands. It is easy for God out of some of these to provide a person to reign over England."

For Aelfflaed, this was enough to make the succession clear. Cuthbert had agreed metaphorically to anoint her half-brother, who was in hiding over the sea in Ireland.

She then asked him a second question: whether Cuthbert would be willing to become bishop, with the implication that he would spiritually oversee the passing of the crown from one of her brothers to another.

"Oh, with what various intentions are the hearts of men distracted!" she chided him. "Some rejoice in having obtained riches, others always eager after them are still in want: but thou rejectest the glory of the world, although it is offered thee, and although thou mightest obtain a bishopric, than which there is

nothing more sublime on earth, yet thou preferrest the recesses of
thy desert to this rank."

"I know that I am not worthy of so high a rank," he replied
carefully, "nevertheless, I cannot shun the judgement of the Supreme
Ruler, who, if he decreed that I should subject myself to so great a
burden, would, I believe, restore me after a moderate freedom, and
perhaps after not more than two years would send me back to my
former solitude and quiet."

So, on Coquet Island, in 684, a deal was done between this
influential man and this influential woman, between the hermit and
the princess. Cuthbert would give his authority to the succession
and, in return, he would only have to serve for two years as bishop.

It was not an easy burden, but he made a success of it—both
politically and spiritually. He was so close to power that he was with
Aelfflaed's sister-in-law the Queen when, as he had predicted, the
king died. And although there is no record of Cuthbert's role in the
succession, Aelfflaed's half-brother ruled for almost twenty years,
starting what would eventually become known as the golden age
of the Kingdom of Northumbria. Cuthbert made a success too of
being both bishop and hermit.

This is what his other biographer, an anonymous monk and
near-contemporary, says of his time as bishop:

> He continued with the utmost constancy to be what he had been
> before; he showed the same humility of heart, the same poverty
> of dress, and, being full of authority and grace, he maintained the
> dignity of a bishop without abandoning the ideal of the monk or the
> virtue of the hermit . . . For his discourse was pure and frank, full
> of gravity and probity, full of sweetness and grace . . . To each one
> he gave varied advice with exhortations suitable to his character;
> that is to say he always knew beforehand what advice to give to
> any man and when and how it should be given.[2]

He was strict too, as a hermit-bishop would be. There are hints—in the reference to the poverty of dress and in his refusal to wear the cloth that the Abbess Verca gave him while he was alive—that there was a tendency for these Anglo-Saxon monasteries to be less like places of religious discipline and more a spiritual retreat for aristocrats, some of whom were unwilling to swap their rich, soft, ostentatious clothing for scratchy, undyed wool. Perhaps even that final question—"Tell us, my Lord Bishop, when we may hope for your return?"—was not that of a faithful servant but a cruel taunt to remind a sick, old man that he had no option but to die a hard, lonely death.

Cuthbert's last act as bishop was to visit two of the leading women of the church: one was the Abbess Verca and the other was Aelfflaed.

Aefflaed had asked him to dedicate a new church for her at Ovington. Yet, on this their last meeting, something so strange happened that she was to tell the anonymous biographer about it.

On that day, Cuthbert fell into a trance while they were dining. This unnamed monk's account differs from that of Bede in some details, but the shape of the story is the same. Cuthbert experienced a *petit mal*; his limbs relaxed, his colour changed, his hand lost its grip on his knife which clattered onto the table, his eyes were "unusually fixed".

His priest leaned in to alert Aelfflaed to his incapacitation, and when Cuthbert came to, she asked him what had been revealed to him in his moment of reverie. At first, Cuthbert tried to laugh off the dropped knife.

But she was intrigued. She pressed him further.

Eventually, he told her that while in his trance he had seen a soul being carried to heaven.

"From what place was it taken?" she asked.

"From your monastery," he replied.

And his name?

"*You* will tell it me," said Cuthbert finally, "tomorrow when I am celebrating mass."

Aelfflaed sent a messenger out overnight to find someone whose passing could confirm Cuthbert's second-sight, and, back on her estate, the messenger discovered how a shepherd called Hadwald had died that day, having fallen out of a tree.

According to the anonymous biographer, when the messenger returned the next day, it was just in time for Aelfflaed to burst in to the middle of the mass and reveal what had happened. She rushed in at the very point when Cuthbert was asking God to remember the souls of the departed—as dramatic a moment as an objection in the middle of a wedding.

"Remember, Lord, thy servants . . . " Cuthbert intoned.

Breathless with excitement, Aelfflaed revealed what she has found out. She delivered the news, Bede records, with woman-like astonishment, "as if she were going to tell him something new and doubtful".

"I pray, my lord bishop, remember in the mass my servant Hadwald, who died yesterday by falling from a tree."

But Bede is also recording something more than her excitement at being the person to reveal how the prophesy had been fulfilled. Perhaps there is a hint of flirty incredulity that the passing of so low a soul should have been shown to so high a bishop.

So, something happened at the dedication of the church in Ovington—some public drama between this man and this woman in the drama of the mass. At their moment of parting, as he left her for the last time before his death, something occurred that was memorable enough to be recalled in subtly different versions by different witnesses some twenty years later.

It is unlikely they ever saw each other again. Cuthbert returned to Inner Farne to die. This is what Herefrith told Bede.

His malady now began to grow upon him, and we thought that the time of his dissolution was at hand. He bade his attendants carry him to his cell and oratory. It was the third hour of the day. We therefore carried him thither, for he was too feeble to walk himself. When we reached the door, we asked him to let one of us go in with him to wait upon him: for no one had ever entered therein but himself. He cast his eyes round on all, and fixing them on the sick brother, above mentioned, said, "Wahlstod shall go in with me."

Now Wahlstod was the man's name. He went in accordingly, and stayed till the ninth hour; when he came out, and said to me, "The bishop wishes you to go in unto him; but I have a most wonderful thing to tell you: from the moment of my touching the bishop, when I supported him into the oratory, I have been entirely free from my old complaint."

No doubt this was brought about by the effect of his heavenly piety, that, whereas in his time of health and strength he had healed many, he should now heal this man, when he was himself at the point of death, that so there might be a standing proof how strong the holy man was in spirit, though his body was at the lowest degree of weakness . . .

I went in to him about the ninth hour of the day, and found him lying in one corner of his oratory before the altar. I took my seat by his side, but he spoke very little, for the weight of his suffering prevented him from speaking much. But when I earnestly asked him what last discourse and valedictory salutation he would bequeath to the brethren, he began to make a few strong admonitions respecting peace and humility, and told me to beware of those persons who strove against these virtues, and would not practise them.

Bede recorded Cuthbert's last words which were delivered "at intervals, for, as we before said, the violence of his complaint had taken from him the power of speaking much at once". However, unlike the rest of Herefrith's story, there are aspects of Cuthbert's deathbed speech that sound as they have been written to suit later circumstances, particularly what he says about moving his bones.

"Have peace," said he, "and divine charity ever amongst you: and when you are called upon to deliberate on your condition, see that you be unanimous in council. Let concord be mutual between you and other servants of Christ; and do not despise others who belong to the faith and come to you for hospitality, but admit them familiarly and kindly; and when you have entertained them, speed them on their journey: by no means esteeming yourselves better than the rest of those who partake of the same faith and mode of life. But have no communion with those who err from the unity of the Catholic faith, either by keeping Easter at an improper time, or by their perverse life. And know and remember that, if of two evils you are compelled to choose one, I would rather that you should take up my bones, and leave these places, to reside wherever God may send you, than consent in any way to the wickedness of schismatics, and so place a yoke upon your necks. Study diligently, and carefully observe the Catholic rules of the fathers, and practise with zeal those institutes of the monastic life which it has pleased God to deliver to you through my ministry. For I know that, although during my life some have despised me, yet after my death you will see what sort of man I was, and that my doctrine was by no means worthy of contempt."

He then spent the rest of the day until the evening in the expectation of future happiness; to which he added this also, that he spent the night in watchfulness and prayer.

When his hour of evening service was come, he received from me the blessed sacrament, and thus strengthened himself for his departure, which he now knew to be at hand, by partaking of the body and blood of Christ; and when he had lifted up his eyes to heaven, and stretched out his hands above him, his soul, intent upon heavenly praises, sped his way to the joys of the heavenly kingdom.

It was 20 March 687.

Lighting two torches that were standing ready, a waiting monk ran to the highest point of the island to wave them into the night. It was the signal agreed with the monastery on Lindisfarne, although it might just as easily have been a signal to the citadel at Bamburgh.

"He was carried by ship to our island," wrote the anonymous biographer, "but first his whole body was washed, his head wrapped in a head cloth and an obley [communion bread, probably contained in a small, wooden altar that he had used in his missionary work] placed upon his holy breast. He was robed in his priestly garments, wearing his shoes in readiness to meet Christ and provided with a waxed shroud."

No one recorded the final act, but after his body had been washed, someone also put a piece of gold jewellery around Cuthbert's neck. It was a small, exquisite pectoral cross made of beaten gold and garnets—the garnets the red of drying blood. The shape of this cross, its narrow curving arms forming the same tight circles, can be seen in the patterns of the Lindisfarne Gospels[3] and on ornate book plates made from gilt bronze used at Whitby Abbey, Aelfflaed's home.[4]

"The body of the venerable father was . . . met by a large crowd of persons singing psalms," Herefrith told Bede, "and placed in the church of the holy Apostle Peter, in a stone coffin on the right hand side of the altar."

CHAPTER TWO

The Body that Would Not Rot

20 March 698 (eleven years after Cuthbert's death)

> After eleven years, through the prompting and instruction of the
> Holy Spirit, after a council had been held by the elders and licence
> had been given by the holy Bishop Eadberht, the most faithful men
> of the whole congregation decided to raise the relics of the bones
> of the holy Bishop Cuthbert from his sepulchre.

This is the anonymous biographer, but according to Bede, the
Lindisfarne carpenters had first been asked to create an ornate
reliquary to hold and venerate Cuthbert's bones. They built a coffin-
shaped box, made from six planks cut from a single, slow growing
oak tree that had seeded three- to four-hundred years before, in
the time of the Romans. Straight and even in grain, it was probably
cleaved rather than sawn into planks. The carpenters used shell
augers with tapering ends to drill the holes for the pegs that would
hold the reliquary together, and they packed the rebates with wool-
tow where they were loose. Then they carved images on the outside.

Down one long side and on one of the ends they inscribed seven
archangels; the choice taken from the liturgy of the Irish church,
from which tradition Cuthbert had come. Down the other long side,
they inscribed the twelve apostles—the followers of Jesus—and on
the remaining end, they carved Jesus as a baby in the arms of his
mother. On the lid, which was slightly larger than the chest, they
chose an image of an adult but beardless Jesus surrounded by the
symbols of the four gospel writers: an angel, a lion, an ox and an eagle.

Two men worked on the carving. One had more artistic skill than the other, or worked the tools better. They started by scoring out the carvings with a knife. Then one of them used a gouge with a semi-circular cutting surface to create the rounded, rebated lines of the figures while the other, more relaxed and more flowing in his style, continued to use a knife, cutting out deep V-shaped grooves. At one point, the gouger, having marked out the hair and the face of the final archangel to the right on the long side, swapped with the knife carver, or he swapped tools, because the fifth angel is finished with a knife. And they were copying something, something that aimed at the naturalistic, showing men in loose Mediterranean clothes and in noble, classical attitudes. The carvers bodged it, a little. They did not seem to have understood how the clothing works—those loose-fitting toga-like tunics with their draping folds. Perhaps they did not understand how the art they were copying had been informed by perspective. Perhaps when they were finished they also painted the reliquary, adding borders of tiny beasts and flowers.

The monastery did this because the monks were now aware that the remnants of Cuthbert's earthly life had power. The shoes he had worn in life healed people; the soil into which they poured the water that had been used to prepare his body for burial healed people; the calfskin hide that had repaired the roof of his oratory on Inner Farne—they all healed people. Just as he had healed people while he was alive, just as he had healed Walhstod in his final days.

So why would the monks not have chosen to disinter his bones, in order to get closer to that power, to bring it to the surface, to make it work more efficiently for their community?

However, they did not find what they were expecting. And once again there are two records of what happened when they disinterred Cuthbert's body, one by his anonymous near-contemporary, the other by Bede, who was then thirty years old. This is the anonymous version.

And, on first opening the sepulchre, they found a thing marvellous to relate, namely that the whole body was as undecayed as when they had buried it eleven years before. The skin had not decayed nor grown old, nor the sinews become dry, making the body tautly stretched and stiff; but the limbs lay at rest with all the appearance of life and were still moveable at the joints. For his neck and knees were like those of a living man, and when they lifted him from the tomb they could bend him as they wished. None of his vestments and footwear which touched the flesh of his body was worn away.

They unwound the head cloth in which his head was wrapped and found that it kept all the beauty of its first whiteness; and the new shoes, with which he was shod, are preserved in our church over against the relics, for a testimony, up to this present day.

It is the whiteness of the vestments and wrappings that so astounded them, and the disconcerting flexibility of the body. It is common to the two accounts, and oddly, both mention the skin, not the face, of the man the monks knew in life. Perhaps the face was bandaged. Certainly, the unwrapping of the head cloth sounds like some form of mummification.

And, as will happen again in the story of Cuthbert's corpse, when they disinterred the body, the bishop was not there.

On 20 March 698, the bishop was in retreat. He was on the tiny nub of grassy rock on that Lindisfarne shore that is still called Cuthbert's Isle. It is a kind of natural hermitage, an anchorite's islet, just down the escarpment from the church. You could wade across, or hit it with a stone, you could shout the news over when the tide was too high. It was the place Cuthbert first retreated to before he went to the severe isolation of Inner Farne.

This was Cuthbert's successor, on Cuthbert's Isle, no more than hailing distance across the sound, but he was not there on the day they disinterred Cuthbert's bones. Bede explains:

As a proof of the uncorrupted state of the clothes, they took a portion of them from one of the extremities, for they did not dare to take any from the body itself, and hastened to tell what they had found to the bishop, who was then walking alone at a spot remote from the monastery, and closed in by the flowing waves of the sea. Here it was his custom to pass the Quadragesima [the first Sunday in Lent]; and here he occupied himself forty days before the birthday of our Lord in the utmost devotion, accompanied with abstinence, prayer, and tears. Here, also, his venerable predecessor Cuthbert, before he went to Farne, as we have related, spent a portion of his spiritual warfare in the service of the Lord. The brethren brought with them, also, the piece of cloth in which the body of the saint had been wrapped. The bishop thanked them for the gift, and heard their report with eagerness, and with great earnestness kissed the cloth as if it were still on the saint's body.

"Fold up the body," said he, "in new cloth instead of this, and place it in the chest which you have prepared. But I know of a certainty that the place which has been consecrated by the virtue of this heavenly miracle will not long remain empty . . . "

And maybe Bede is right. Maybe they had made the reliquary before they discovered the body was whole. Because the coffin-reliquary was just too short and the monks had to lay Cuthbert on his side, a little folded up. Perhaps this accounts for some of the hurry with the carving. Or perhaps the planks had already been delivered for a reliquary and then they discovered they needed a coffin. And with the life-like corpse waiting—perhaps in the church, perhaps in some kind of vestry, who might not bodge it in his hurry? Finally, as Bede records:

With many tears and much contrition, the brethren did as [the bishop] ordered them; and having folded up the body in some new cloth, and placed it in a chest, laid it on the pavement of the sanctuary.

CHAPTER THREE

The First Anglo-Saxon Kings of All England

c. 934 (247 years after Cuthbert's death)

Why would you not go to Lindisfarne? In a world where illness was not understood, why would you not go to place your fragile self or hold your sick child near such power?

In the years immediately after the discovery, the biographies written by the anonymous monk and by Bede were copied and sent around England and Europe. Their work announced the miracle of Cuthbert's incorrupt corpse, and it became widely known that in the north of England, across the tidal flats of an island called Lindisfarne, there lay the body of a man so perfectly devout that the mechanisms of death itself had been put on hold by the pure intensity of his faith.

Instead of a cadaver seething with corruption, his corpse was as close to a living man as a dead mortal could become. So why would you not go to Lindisfarne? If his body did not obey the laws of corruption, it must mean the saint was close to God and so could intercede on your behalf. If his body did not decompose, it must be radiating a power that could hold the horrors of disease and corruption at bay. So, if you could, why would you *not* go to bathe in such a life-giving emanation?

And, naturally, along with their desire to be well and whole, the pilgrims brought items to exchange, because they had to live and rest and eat while they were on pilgrimage. So it was understandable that it would be the monks they would turn to for these necessities.

Along with their barter-goods and coins, the pilgrims also brought gifts—sometimes gold and jewellery, sometimes gifts of land—which they could exchange for spiritual wealth, both in the here-and-now and in the hereafter. So in the hundred or so years after the death of Cuthbert, the monastery and its monks, however sincere their intentions, grew rich.

It was this wealth, and their vulnerability to the sea, that also attracted the Vikings, and Lindisfarne became the first place in England to be raided. This is the Anglo-Saxon Chronicle for the year 793:

> In this year dire forewarnings came over the land of the Northumbrians, and miserably terrified the people: there were excessive whirlwinds and lightnings, and fiery dragons were seen flying in the air. A great famine soon followed these tokens, and a little after that, in the same year, on the sixth of the Ides of January, the havoc of heathen men miserably destroyed God's church on Lindisfarne, through rapine and slaughter.[5]

And this is the monastic community's memory of the event, as it was recorded 300 years later:

> The pagans from the Northern region came with a naval armament to Britain, like stinging hornets, and overran the country in all directions, like fierce wolves, plundering, tearing, and killing not only sheep and oxen, but priests and Levites [assistants], and choirs of monks and nuns. They came, as we before said, to the church of Lindisfarne, and laid all waste with dreadful havoc, trod with unhallowed feet the holy places, dug up the altars, and carried off all the treasures of the holy church. Some of the brethren they killed; some they carried off in chains; many they cast out, naked and loaded with insults; some they drowned in the sea.[6]

Over the next 150 years, first through raids and then though invasion and settlement, the Vikings carved apart the Northumbrian kingdom that Bede, Aelfflaed and Cuthbert had helped to create.

First, the onslaught destroyed record keeping and history. There was now no reliable Bede-like authority seeking to record and order the world around him in cloistered security. From this point until the eleventh century, the corpse entered a period of legend. And there was no one like Aelfflaed, working her diplomatic connections between the monasteries and the rulers, helping each to help the other. Indeed, Aelfflaed's royal house and her kingdom were to disappear under the Viking onslaught, leaving the monastery on its own. There was no longer any profit to being on Lindisfarne where, instead of the opportunity to grow rich from the pilgrims and the sea-going trade, they were now always vulnerable.

As a consequence, in the spring of 875 and after decades of attacks, the monastery took the decision to leave Lindisfarne in order to find a place of safety inland. The monks dismantled the timbers of their first church and packed them onto carts; they lugged their ancient stone cross out of the ground and added it to the load. They dug up and disinterred the bones of their founder and their previous bishops, packing alongside these relics the battle-cracked skull of King Oswald, Aelfflaed's uncle. With great reverence, they secured the wonder of their gospel book, with its intricate designs, brilliant colours and perfect calligraphy. Finally, they prepared a great chest, a travelling coffin covered in hides to guard against the elements. This would transport the now antique coffin-reliquary, concealed within whose angelic, apostolic carvings lay the community's most precious and revered essence: the miracle-working, sanctuary-granting, divine portal that was the incorrupt corpse of St Cuthbert.

A praetorian guard of seven young monks was chosen to protect and attend to the corpse on its journey. It was a responsibility so great that the seven were to become heroes, and their descendants were to be venerated for generations. We still know some of their names: Hunred, Stitheard, Edmund and Franco.

The great procession would surely have sung and lamented as it crossed the strand on to the mainland, just as the monks sang to greet Cuthbert's body on its return from Farne. Carrying everything with them that made them a monastery, surrounded by their families, their retainers and their livestock, the monks left Lindisfarne to join the muddy, cobble-strewn scar that marked the vestiges of the old Roman road.

The legend that has come down to us is that this is a journey of flight and fear in which a desperate, dwindling band of true believers, their monastic discipline dying on the road, hid out in the swamps and forests of the north from the pagan invaders.

But through the breakdown of record keeping and secular authority, it's possible to sense that the monastery was doing something much more strategic. The monks appear to be taking the one thing that gave them their power—the incorrupt corpse—and transporting it to the places where that power could have the most impact: to the lands that have been given as gifts to Cuthbert and which they needed to secure.

In a complex seven-year series of movements across the north of England, the corpse and its guardians went through a succession of relocations. In fits and starts, the corpse was first taken west to Norham, then back to Lindisfarne, then further west to Whithorn, and the mouth of the Derwent on the Irish Sea coast. Next they turn south-east to Crayke, before establishing themselves, around 883, in the possibly still-defensible remains of the old Roman fort at Chester-le-Street.

It is likely no coincidence that the geography of this journey sketches out the land holdings of the Lindisfarne monastery within the vestiges of the Kingdom of Northumbria. Instead of flight and fear, the sequence of relocations can be seen as a tactical withdrawal followed by a royal progress through their lands. The monastery seems to be engaged in a series of strategic visitations to its estates; visitations in which the coffin is presented like a crown or a seal, as a symbol of over-lordship as powerful as if the saint himself were present.

But what is most telling is that apart from the journey west to the Irish Sea coast, which is associated in legend with an attempt to flee to Ireland, the community spent much of its time taking the corpse *towards* the Viking areas of control. They engaged with the invaders and they secured their legacy.

So we hear of them in York around 883, where the presence of the saint's body sanctified the election of a former slave named Guthred to the Viking kingship: an alliance that granted the community control over all the land between the Tyne and the Wear.

And when the resurgent Anglo-Saxon kings do eventually return to the north in the middle of the tenth century, one element of the old Kingdom of Northumbria remains. Aelfflaed's royal house may not have survived, but it is the corpse of Cuthbert to which the victorious House of Wessex come to pay penance. It is the heirs of King Alfred who come to Chester-le-Street, to bring tribute to the political and feudal power embodied by the corpse.

So important is this alliance between the northern monks and the southern court that, in return for their homage, these first kings of all-England are granted the right to do more than merely place themselves near the coffin-reliquary and experience the emanation from the saint. For them, the monks will open the hide-bound travelling chest, they will lift the carved lid of the coffin-reliquary, and they will allow their royal visitors to place their gifts next to, and even on, the body of the saint.

The events are recorded in the *Historia de sancto Cuthberto*, a chronicle written almost one hundred years later.

At that time King Edward, full of days and worn down by ripe old age, summoned his son Aethelstan, handed his kingdom over to him, and diligently instructed him to love Saint Cuthbert and honour him above all saints, revealing to him he how he had mercifully succoured his father King Alfred in poverty and exile and how he had boldly aided him against all enemies, and in what way he had always very clearly come most promptly as his continual helper whenever there was need. After making this admonition, he happily died.

Therefore, while King Aethelstan was leading a great army from the south to the northern region, taking it to Scotland, he made a diversion to the church of Saint Cuthbert and gave royal gifts to him, and then composed and signed a testament and placed it at Saint Cuthbert's head.

"In the name of our Lord Jesus Christ, I, King Aethelstan, give to Saint Cuthbert this gospel-book, two chausbles, and one alb, and one stole with maniple, and one belt, and three altar-coverings, and one silver chalice, and two patens, one finished with gold, the other of Greek workmanship, and one sliver thurible, and one cross skilfully finished with gold and ivory, and one royal headdress woven with gold, and two tables crafted of silver and gold, and two silver candelabra finished with gold, and one missal, and two gospel-books ornamented with gold and silver and one life of Saint Cuthbert written in verse and in prose, and seven palls, and three curtains, and three tapestries, and two silver cups with covers, and four large bells, and three horns crafted of gold and silver, and two banners, and one lance, and two golden amulets, and my beloved vill of Bishop Wearmouth with its dependencies, namely Westun, Offferton, Silsworth, the two Ryhopes, Burdon, Seham, Seaton, Dalton-le-Dale, Dawdon, Cold Hesledon. All these I give under witness of God and Saint Cuthbert, so that if anyone steals anything there, let him be damned on the Day of Judgement with the traitor Judas and be thrust 'into everlasting fire which was prepared for the devil and his angels.'"

He also filled the aforementioned cups with the best coin, and at his order his whole army offered Saint Cuthbert twelve hundred [shillings?] and more. Then he fraternally instructed his brother Edmund, who had already been informed of the sanctity and faithful patronage of the holy confessor, that if anything sinister should befall him on this expedition to return his body to Saint Cuthbert and commends it to him for presentation to God on the Day of Judgement. After this he departed, fought happily, returned successfully, ruled wisely for many years afterwards and at last died happily.

When he died his brother Edmund succeeded to the kingdom, again gathered a great army and hastened to Scotland. On the way however, he made a diversion to the church of Saint Cuthbert, knelt before his tomb, poured out prayers, and commended himself and his men to God and the holy confessor; the army offered sixty pounds, while he himself with his own hand, placed two gold amulets and two Greek palls upon the holy body . . . [7]

This was the triumph of the community. So skilfully have they used the power of the corpse to negotiate the Viking invasion that they emerged more powerful than they were before; and the first kings of all England, the House of Wessex, had to come to Chester-le-Street and bring tribute.

CHAPTER FOUR

The Coming of the Normans

*29 August 1104 (417 years, five months and
nine days after Cuthbert's death)*

It was not the Normans who moved Cuthbert's corpse to Durham, but their Anglo-Saxon predecessors. After just over a century in Chester-le-Street, they must have seen in this final resting place a fitting site. A hill surrounded on three sides by a deep, looping river gorge, it was imposing *and* defensible. After the Vikings, defensibility mattered. But perhaps they also found it fitting because it symbolised their origins. In their mind's eye, the hill encircled by the river would have reminded them of Lindisfarne and how it too was looped in by water: by a circling of the floodtide that only closed itself around the island twice a day. Perhaps they even saw further—back across the sea to the Irish origins of Cuthbert's Christianity and to the very beginnings of Celtic spirituality: to the mystical in the water.

The Normans may not have chosen Durham but they did make it permanent. They began building the Cathedral in 1093, and the creation of this vast mausoleum put a monumental end to the Anglo-Saxon concept that the corpse could travel. However, unlike the monarchy and earldoms of England, the Normans could not simply usurp the native incumbents with violence. In the north, it was the entity called St Cuthbert who was the local lord, and, as incorrupt as Cuthbert's corpse was, it was already dead. In this context, the Normans therefore had to justify the transfer of sovereignty, and they did this by writing their own history of the corpse. The man chosen to create the Norman narrative was a monk called Symeon. He seems to have come over from Normandy in 1091 and rose to become the chief scribe at the monastery. Among other tasks, we know he copied out the Durham versions of Bede's life of Cuthbert, compiled various annals and generally made himself an expert on the history of the monastery. All of this was preparation for his great justificatory narrative "A Tract on the Origins and Progress of this the Church of Durham"[8]—the book that demonstrated that the Norman guardianship of Cuthbert's legacy was legitimate because they were restoring Cuthbert to the true, Benedictine tradition of real monks.

So instead of seeing the Anglo-Saxon guardians as sophisticated power brokers, securing their lands during the dislocation of the Viking attacks, Symeon's tract presented them as fleeing in terror and dwindling to a small band of hereditary priests, or clerks, as he dismissively called them. They were no longer monks in anything but name, he implies: they may have sung like monks, but they raised children like ordinary men.

Most of the famous Cuthbert legends come from his version of the corpse's history: the flight to Ireland, the dropping of the Lindisfarne Gospels into the water, the saint turning the sea red to indicate his displeasure at their attempt to escape England. It is Symeon who emphasises the guardians' almost accidental role in the founding of Durham—the milkmaid, the dun cow, the cart carrying the coffin getting caught in the mire. In this way the inheritors of Bede, Cuthbert and Aelfflaed—the creators of the Lindisfarne Gospels, the astute politicians of the Viking age, who received tribute from the heirs of King Alfred—are turned into clumsy, suggestible cart-hands, unworthy of the possession of such profound power.

Symeon's book, however, was only a kind of prequel; a justificatory companion volume to the profound, symbolic and public ceremony of the coffin's transference to its ultimately permanent, immovable encasement in the new cathedral. As if to underline the point, on the day of what is known as the translation, 29 August 1104, the Norman guardians paraded the coffin outside for one last time.

This is how one chronicler, William of Malmesbury, described the event:

> The sight was a splendid one—the church-yard was the scene; the sky was clear, no black cloud deadened the beams of the sun, the monks were all arrayed in the robes of their order, and there were long lines of men going and returning, treading, in fact, upon each other's heels, from their intense anxiety to view again and again the sight which they had seen. But . . . there came at once a mighty and unlooked-for shower, which drove the whole assembly into the church.[9]

Perhaps it was a triumphant burlesque, this taking the coffin outside and marching it around their vast new building. Perhaps in some way the Normans were aping their Anglo-Saxon predecessors, with their tiny wooden churches and their pathetic parading of the body around their lands like the waving of a document.

Taking the coffin out to the waiting crowds, trampling over each other in their excitement, created a public statement of power and exultation: We possess the body; the miracle of the incorrupt corpse is ours.

Symeon knew this for a fact because, five days before, he had been part of a secret investigation into the coffin's contents. Once again, there are two accounts of what happened, which mirror the two recordings of the first discovery on Lindisfarne centuries before. One is by an anonymous monk who was most likely part of the monastery at the time, and the other is by a historian called Reginald. Like his predecessor Bede, Reginald was working some years later, relying on interviews with the elders of the monastery who had themselves spoken to witnesses: "men who had touched with their hands the incorruptible body of Saint Cuthbert, had explored it with their stead-fast eyes, had lifted it up and sustained it with their clasping arms, and they had learnt every secret concerning him . . .

These men related to their hearers the mighty deeds of God, and made them better acquainted with certain matters which before were secret, and yet they were unwilling to commit the whole to writing."[10]

The main account is by the anonymous monk.

24 August 1104

Under the head of miracles, all do not entertain one and the same opinion, either with respect to the presence of the sacred body of Saint Cuthbert, or its state of incorruption. Some, founding their opinion on various conjectures, dream that before this our time his body has been removed to some other place, but that his grave, although it can no longer boast of its occupant, is not deprived of the glory of his virtues; but, in proof of its old possessor, gives frequent miraculous manifestations even at the present time.

Others admit that the sacred remains are still here, but, that the frame of a human body should remain undissolved during the revolutions of so many ages, is more than the laws of nature allow of; and that notwithstanding the Divine Power may command all created things to undergo its pleasure, yet that in the case of this body, and its state of incorruption, they have before them the testimony of no one who had explored it either with his hand or eye, and that therefore it was a difficult matter to believe with respect to this man, however much a saint—a thing not in his case proved, and which they were well aware had been conceded to a very few only of holy men.

In this manner the one party conjecturing that the holy body had been carried away elsewhere, and the other not allowing its incorruption, the brethren who affirmed that it was there, and in a perfect state, were disbelieved, and they became in consequence anxious for their reputation.

On this account they betook themselves to God in prayer, and entreated that He, who is wonderful in his saints, would prove himself wonderful in the manifestation of so great virtue, and would, to the glory of his name, exclude all doubt by indubitable signs. In the meanwhile, the Church which had been founded by William, the late Bishop of Durham, was almost finished, and the time was at hand for transferring into it the venerable body of Father Cuthbert, to occupy the place prepared for it by the ingenious hands of workmen, and receive the meed of worthy veneration.

29 August, the day appointed for the solemn removal, being at hand, the brethren entered into a resolution, that as no one was alive who could give them accurate information, they themselves, as far as they should be allowed by the permission of God, should examine into the manner in which each individual thing was placed and arranged about the holy body, for this purpose, that they might make it ready for removal on the day approaching, and without loss of time furnish it with things fit and becoming, lest when the hour of festive procession had arrived, any difficulty, proceeding from want of foresight, should cause delay, and from that delay any unpleasant feeling should arise in the minds of the numerous assemblage which had come together to witness such a solemnity. The brethren, therefore, appointed for the purpose, nine in number, with Turgot their Prior, having qualified themselves for the task by fasting and prayer, on 24 August, as soon as it was dark, prostrated themselves before the venerable coffin, and amid tears and prayers they tried to open it with fearful and trembling hands.

According to Reginald, the outer encasement was an ornamental box, decorated with gold and precious stones.

Aided by instruments of iron, they soon succeeded in their attempt, when, to their astonishment, they found a chest covered on all sides with hides, carefully fixed to it by iron nails. From the weight and size of this chest, and other facts which presented themselves, they were induced to believe that there was another coffin within it, but fear for a long time prevented them from making the experiment. At last, the Prior having twice or thrice commanded them to proceed, they renewed their task, and having succeeded in opening the iron bands, they lifted up the lid.

Here they saw within, a coffin of wood, which had been covered all over by coarse linen cloth of a threefold texture, of the length of a man, and covered with a lid of the same description. Again they hesitated, for a doubt arose, whether this was the dwelling-place of the holy body, or that there was still another coffin within. In this stage of their operations, they called to mind the words of Bede, which record that the body of Saint Cuthbert had been found by the brethren of Lindisfarne in a state of incorruption, eleven years after its burial, and had been placed above ground for the purpose of worthy veneration. With this information before them, they discovered that this was the very same coffin, which had for so many years preserved the deposit of so heavenly a treasure . . .

[The coffin] was quadrangular like a chest, and its lid is not elevated in the middle, but flat, so that its summit, whether of lid or sides, is all along level and even. The lid is like the lid of a box, broad and flat. The lid itself is a tablet of wood, serving for an opening, and the whole of it is made to be lifted up by means of two circles or rings, which are fixed in its midway breadth, the one in the direction of his feet, and the other in that of his head. By these rings the lid is elevated and let down, and there is no lock or fastening whatever to attach it to the coffin. The coffin is made entirely of black oak, and it may be doubted whether it was contracted that colour of blackness from old age, from some device, or from nature. The whole of it is externally carved with very admirable engraving, of such minute and most delicate work, that the beholder, instead of admiring the skill or powers of the carver, is lost in amazement. The compartments are very circumscribed and small, and they are occupied by divers beasts, flowers, and images, which seem to be inserted, engraved, or furrowed out in the wood.

Realising that they have now far more proof of the likelihood of the body being there than they did before, the monks paused and some of their resolve disappeared. Opening an ornate box was one thing; discovering the Anglo-Saxon coffin mentioned by Bede put them in a much more significant position. The anonymous monk continues the story.

> Under this conviction they fell upon their knees and prayed Saint Cuthbert to intercede with the Almighty for pardon for their presumption. They rejoiced, and at the same time they were afraid. Their fear resulted from an apprehension of the consequences of their boldness, and yet, the certainty that they had before them so great a treasure inspiring them with delight, their joy burst forth into tears, and with thankful hearts they conceived that their desires had been amply satisfied.
>
> To make a further examination appeared to be a rashness, which would unquestionably bring down upon them the Divine vengeance; and, therefore, laying aside their intention to more minutely investigating the sacred body, they entered into deliberation as to the manner in which it should be removed on the day of translation which was approaching.

In the dark vault of the new Cathedral, the possibilities and responsibilities must have been terrifying and it is believable that they lost their resolve. Not only were they close to the very thing that provided the *raison d'être* for the upcoming ceremony, the investment in the new mausoleum as well as their usurpation of the temporal power built up by the Anglo-Saxon guardians of the corpse. They were also as close as it was possible for a man to get to the power of the resurrection: to a body that was dead but not decayed. It is no wonder they hesitated.

> But amongst the brethren who were present, there was one, a man of great constancy in Christ, who, by the effect of grace, had become that in fact which his name implied. His name was Leofwin, which means, in English, a dear friend. He was dear to God, and God was a friend to him.
>
> He, when he saw the brethren afraid of opening the coffin which they had discovered, and viewing the proof of celestial grace and matter of new exultation which it might contain, stepped forward into the midst of them, and speaking in a more fervent spirit than was his custom, exclaimed, "What do ye, my brethren! What do ye fear? That deed will never fail of being attended by a happy result, which begins from the inspiration of God. He who gave us the will to make the investigation, gives us the hope of discovering what we seek. The progress which we have already made without difficulty, is a proof of the good which we may hope to arise from what remains to be done. Our beginning would never have been so successful, if it had been the Divine will that we should not persevere to the end. God will never set that down to the score of rashness which proceeds from a devout mind. Our object in investigating these sacred relics proceeds from no contempt or diffidence of his holiness, but that the Lord of virtues, the King himself of glory, may be the more glorified by all men in proportion of the mightiness of the miracle manifested in the present day. Let us then examine the inner parts of the hospitable chest, that upon a matter which we have seen with our eyes, and have thoroughly examined, which our hands have handled, our testimony may be credited, and no argument may be left to the doubtful for disbelieving our assertions."

Emboldened by Leofwin's exhortation, the monks proceeded to investigate the Anglo-Saxon coffin.

The devout brethren regained their confidence by this admonition, and moved the venerable body from behind the altar, where it had hitherto reposed, into the middle of the choir—a place more spacious and better adapted to the investigation.

Their first step was to remove the lined cloth which enveloped the coffin, yet still they feared to open the coffin itself; and under a hope that its contents might be ascertained through a chink, or by other means, they carefully examined its exterior by candle-light, but without success. They then, but not without fear, removed the lid, and no sooner had they done this than they found another lid, placed somewhere lower, resting upon three transverse bars, and occupying the whole breadth and length of the coffin, so as completely to conceal the contents beneath. Upon the upper part of it, near the head, there lay a book of the Gospels. This second lid was raisable by means of two iron rings, one at the head, and the other at the feet. A doubt no longer remained. They knew that the object of their search was before them, but still they hesitated to handle it with their hands. They had an eager desire to see and touch that which had been the object of their affections; but fear, resulting from a consciousness of their sins, repelled them from the attempt, and between the two they were kept in such suspense as almost to be ignorant which in reality they preferred.

Whilst they were in this state of doubt, being encouraged by the command of the Prior, and the exhortation of the brother above mentioned, at last they raised the lid, and having removed the linen cloth which had covered the sacred relics immediately beneath it, they smelt an odour of the sweetest fragrancy; and behold, they found the venerable body of the blessed Father, the fruit of their anxious desire, laying on its right side in a perfect state, and, from the flexibility of its joints, representing a person asleep rather than dead.

The moment they saw this, a tremendous fear thrilled through their limbs, and they shrunk back to a distance, not daring to look at the miracle before their eyes. Oft and many a time they fell upon their knees, beating their breasts, and exclaiming, with eyes and hands raised to heaven, "Lord have mercy upon us, have mercy upon us."

Whilst they were in this stage, each related to the one who was nearest to him what he had seen, just as if he had been the only one favoured with the sight. After a short interval, they all fell flat on the ground, and amid a deluge of tears, repeated the seven penitential psalms, and prayed the Lord not to correct them in his anger, nor chasten them in his displeasure. When this was done, approaching the coffin on their hands and knees, rather than on their feet, they found in it such a mass of holy relics, that the moderate size of the coffin could never have contained them had not the holy body of the Father, by reclining upon its right side, as has been already mentioned, allowed them on this side and on that a larger portion of space for reposing along with him.

These relics, as is gathered from old books, consisted of the head of the glorious King and Martyr Oswald, the bones of the venerable Confessors of Christ and Priests Aidan, and of (the successors of the venerable Father Cuthbert) Eadbert, Eadfrid, and Ethelwold. There were, besides, the bones of the venerable Bede, who had well written the Life of Saint Cuthbert—these had obtained a resting-place by his side, and along with the rest were contained in a small linen sack . . .

Faced with the prospect of direct contact with the miracle of incorruption, the monks again rely on Leofwin to lead them.

Their first wish was to remove the holy body from its lateral position, and place it on its back; but they were unable to affect this on account of the multitude of relics which surrounded it. They determined, consequently, to remove it altogether for a while, that they might collect and place the relics by themselves, and then restore it to its own proper abode. But still they dreaded to touch it with their hands, until being encouraged by the prayers of the brother above mentioned, they at length became ready to execute the commands of their seniors.

The two deputed to remove the venerable body from the coffin, took their stand, the one at its head and the other at its feet; and whilst they were raising it, holding it by those parts, it began to bend in the middle like a living man, and sink downwards, from its natural weight of solid flesh and bones. A third, upon this, ran up by special command, and supporting its middle in his arms, they reverently placed it upon the pavement upon tapestry and other robes.

"These were the men", writes Reginald: "Turgot the Prior, Alduin the Subprior, Leofwin, Wiking, Godwin and Osbern the Sacrists, Henry, and William, surnamed Havegrun, both of them Archdeacons, Algar afterwards Prior, and Symeon.

"Osbern, in the direction of the head of St Cuthbert, taking hold of the holy body, raised it aloft from the place of its repose; Alduin, standing at the other extremity, elevated the sacred feet; and Algar, when the body was bending to the ground in its middle, after the manner of a living man, seized it and supported it in his arms. (He also assisted the Abbot of Séez in unfolding the vestments which enveloped the venerable head of the Saint.) As soon as the holy body was laid upon tapestry and other robes, Symeon, who held the torch, ceased not to kiss the sacred feet of the body, and moisten them with his tears."

The anonymous chronicler continues:

How did their joy then break forth into tears, what were their words of gratulation, what their exultations of praise, when now at length they had before their eyes that treasure of heavenly grace, in comparison of which even gold itself was of little worth!

They now conceived that they had all things in their possession, when they saw before them, as if alive, him through whom the Divine bounty would bestow upon them the comforts of this present life and the joys of the next.

In the meantime, the relics of the Saints having been removed, they restored the body of the Father to his coffin, with an intention of arranging it in a more decent and becoming manner the following night. The hour of midnight devotion was at hand, and prevented them from lingering any longer over it at present. They, therefore, chanted the *Te Deum* in a low voice, and afterwards, singing psalms of exultation, carried the body back again to the place from which they had removed it.

25 August 1104

That the investigation needed to be done in secret in the night makes some sense. If they had found nothing, or a skeleton, the leadership of the monastery would have needed a different plan for the opening of their Cathedral. But now they could make it public.

When the morning came, the wonderful proceedings of the night were detailed in a full assembly of the brethren, who at first, from the novelty of the event, seemed to be overcome by feelings of stupor: they soon, however, evinced their joy, but it was by tears rather than by words, and on bended knee offered up thanks to Heaven for the favour of being permitted to know that they had such a patron, and for the hope which his merits entitled them to entertain. The Bishop, however, did not easily credit their report, conceiving it altogether incredible that any body, however holy, could, being human, remain free from all taint of corruption for so long a period as four hundred and eighteen years; and an oath would scarcely satisfy him, although taken by men who would have conceived it a crime not to tell the truth even when not under that obligation.

The following night the same brethren who had been present upon the former occasion, in the spirit of humility and with contrite hearts, again brought forth the body into the middle of the choir, and placed it upon robes and tapestry spread upon the pavement. The outer covering was a robe of a costly kind, next below this it was wrapped in a purple dalmatic, and then in linen, and all these swathements retained their original freshness without any stain of corruption. The chasuble, which he had worn for eleven years in his grave, had been removed by the brethren of that period, and is now preserved elsewhere in the church as a proof of incorruption.

Reginald has more information about the state of Cuthbert's corpse: "That body, very admirable for its meritorious virtues, seems to be of a tall and manly stature," he writes, "and yet this tallness is confined within proper bounds. All his limbs, however, are solid, flexible, and whole, and as becomes a perfect man, folding with nerves, moveable with veins full of blood, sweet in the softness of flesh, such as give the appearance of one living in the flesh, rather than dead in the body. His body is everywhere enveloped with a very thinly woven sheet of linen, and between this and the body there is no other interior wrapment. This is the winding sheet which the Abbess Verca gave him during his life-time, and which he always preserved for this very purpose. Next to this he is clothed in a priestly alb, and there appears to be an amice on his neck or shoulders. His cheeks and face, and all the surface or superficies of the whole of his venerable head, are closely covered by a cloth, which is attached to all the parts beneath it with such a degree of anxious care, that it is, as it were, glued to his hair, skin, temples, and beard. Which cloth could in no one part, by the art of any one, be ever so little elevated, torn asunder, or raised from beneath, either from his skin or flesh. Not even by the very sharpest extremity of the nails, was it in any place able to be drawn or pinched up, or in any perceptible degree to be pulled asunder. Through this his nostrils and eyelids were sufficiently clear and visible; but yet the skin below, or the more tender flesh beneath, was not able to be seen distinctly. So also, as far as the joints of his neck, all the functionary parts of the head, and the organs of the sense of man, were in the same manner covered, nor was there, after every attempt, any apparent means by which they could be distinctly viewed. His nose, at its junction with his forehead, seemed to be somewhat turning rapidly outwards; and his chin appeared, to those who saw it, as if the lower bone was furrowed by a two-fold division. In which furrow, so distinct on each side, the quantity of almost a transverse finger might be laid in, because its highest tip was so indented. Above all these there is a purple face-cloth, which conceals and covers beneath it the whole of the mitre upon his head. It does not easily appear of what kind of thread this face-cloth is woven, inasmuch as there is at the present time no such manufacture. Upon the forehead of the holy Bishop there is a fillet of gold, not of woven work, and of gold only externally, which sparkles with most precious stones of different kinds, scattered all over its surface."

Reginald's description of the condition of the corpse is the most detailed of all the accounts, but it should be remembered he is reporting the community's memory of the event over half a century after it happened. He continues:

"Persons devout, rather than curious, who had beheld the sacred interior of his coffin, wishing to view his naked flesh, raised aloft the face-cloth which I have mentioned, and thus between the joints of his neck and the confines of his shoulders saw the softness of his flesh, and handled it with their hands. They saw it, they patted it with their fingers and hands, and found that it was equally consistent over the whole of his body. Above the alb he was decorated with a stole and fanon, the extremities of which are for a short space visible near his feet, but yet no one can ascertain the precise nature of their texture: for their inner parts are covered by the tunic and dalmatic which are above them, but the extremities of their borders appear to be of most costly workmanship . . .

"His hands reclining upon his breast, appear to be extending their stretched-out fingers to heaven, and to be incessantly demanding the mercy of God on behalf of a people devoted to him. For he who, at the hour of his death, raised those hands aloft in prayer on behalf of himself, now since his death, hath ever kept them raised for the expiation of our crimes. And yet those who handle them may move them in any direction, may turn them inwards or outwards with as much ease as if they belonged to a living man. In like manner his arms may be raised and lowered, and all his other limbs may be extended or bent inwards at the will of him who handles them. The chasuble, which was removed from his body eleven years after his burial, was never restored to him afterwards. Upon his feet he wears the episcopal shoes, generally denominated sandals, which in front are perforated with numerous holes, of an exceedingly small size, purposely made. But as to any softer inner garment, or any monk's cowl which he may wear, or may not wear, no one can give any information, because no one ever presumed to touch or explore the robes which are immediately contiguous to his flesh."

The anonymous monk picks up the story:

When, therefore, by examining it with their eyes, by handling it with their hands, by raising it and lowering it, they had clearly discovered that it was a body in a state of incorruption, with solid nerves, and had ascertained that it had been tended with solemn care, in addition to the robes which it already wore, they clothed it with the most costly pall which they could find in the church, and over this they placed a covering of the finest linen. Having wrapped it in these, they restored it to its peaceful abode with the fervent devotion of prayers and tears.

It is not clear when, but at some point over these few days in August 1104, the carpenters in the Cathedral had to do some work on the coffin. Some putrefaction had occurred which had stained and compromised the base of the original Anglo-Saxon reliquary, although Reginald makes very clear that this was not a result of Cuthbert's decomposition.

"When once the sacred body was elevated from the place of its repose," he writes, "the coffin, in which it had hitherto rested reclining upon its right side like one asleep, emitted a fragrant smell of sweetness which filled the air. Even the coffin itself, in which that most sacred body reposed, appeared as fresh as if newly made, and was thoroughly dry. The pillow, made of cloth of costly silk, which had been placed under the body, as far as it had been occupied by it, shone with all the brightness of recent texture.

"But where these relics of [other] Saints had rested, that part of the coffin consigned to them had become black beneath a coagulated mass of decaying dust, and from its long contact with the ashes, had suffered injury, although it still remained entire. Whence it arose, that that part of the chest in which any portion of those holy relics had rested, was filthy, earthy, and somewhat damp. Wherefore they freed the coffin of Saint Cuthbert from these defilements, by collecting together the dust and ashes; and, gathering together the sacred remains themselves, they placed them in certain wooden receptacles, hewn out for the purpose. But because they were not able entirely to scrape off from the part affected, nor eradicate the discolouring caused by the ashes, and the stain proceeding from the moisture, which had sunk deeply down, they had recourse to an artifice for remedying the defect. Their first wish was, if possible, to make the distained part resemble the other perfect parts of the coffin; but this could only be effected by time, and consequently they feared to commence the operation. They, therefore, by a device of their own, made a tablet of wood, of such a size as exactly to correspond with the bottom of the coffin internally in length and breadth: this they dried before the fire from the morning till the evening, and they afterwards besmeared, and, as far as they could, saturated it with melted wax. Their next step was to affix to it, on its lower side four feet, one at each corner, of such a length as, when the thickness of the plank and the length of the feet were taken together, constituted the depth of three fingers only, and by placing this false bottom within the coffin, every part of the real bottom which had been injured by the ashes of the holy relics, was concealed from view. In fact, it had so closely attached itself to the lower bottom of the coffin, that to those who saw it, it appeared to be a new real bottom, lately made smooth by the plane. Its wooden feet beneath supported it upon the old bottom, and effectually concealed all its defects. Upon the upper part of the tablet they placed the incorruptible body of the glorious Bishop in the place of his repose, and the other relics were gathered together and put elsewhere by themselves. Whence it comes to pass, that that most holy body lays not more than half down in its coffin, because it rests not upon the real bottom of the chest, but upon this tablet."

The anonymous monk completes the account of what happened on the second night:

The other things which they had found along with him, they also replaced in his coffin, namely, an ivory comb and a pair of scissors, still retaining their freshness, and, as became a Priest, a silver altar, a linen cloth for covering the sacramental elements, a paten, a chalice, small in size, but from its materials and workmanship, precious, its lower part representing a lion of the purest gold, which bore on its back an onyx stone, made hollow by the most beautiful workmanship, and by the ingenuity of the artist, so attached to the back of the lion, that it might be easily turned round with the hand, although it might not be separated from it. Moreover, of all the relics which had been found there, the only one which they restored to its place, by the side of the glorious Bishop, was the head of the blessed King Oswald. The other relics, as has been already said, which had been removed from thence and decently arranged, are preserved in a frequented part of the church.

As soon as the body of the blessed Father was shut up in the coffin, they covered the coffin itself with linen cloth of a coarse texture, dipped in wax, and restored it to the place behind the altar where it had formerly rested, blessing the Lord of virtues in his deeds, who alone doeth wonderful things, whose mighty works are sought out of all who take pleasures therein.

The nine monks now possessed powerful knowledge. With several days remaining before the ceremony to mark the moving of the body into the new church, they could take their time and consider the possibilities. The Cathedral had been commissioned in order to bring the political power of the Cuthbert community under Norman control. The act of translation, however, concentrated attention on the legend of the incorrupt body and it was likely that others would ask, like the nine monks, whether this Anglo-Saxon saint really did provide a divine mystery for the building to house. Perhaps they understood how impressive it would be if they were obliged to open the coffin and have someone, a sceptic, examine the corpse in public.

29 August 1104

In the mean while, the day of the approaching translation being made known far and wide, there was a great flocking to Durham from every side. Men of all ranks, ages, and professions, the secular and the spiritual, all hastened to be present. They had heard of the miracle, that the body, although dead for so many years, was still free from decay, and they gloried in the fact that such a wonder was made manifest in their time.

Not everyone was convinced however, or appeared to be.

But among the Abbots who had assembled, there was one, who hearing what had taken place, openly complained of the injury which had been done him, and charged the brethren of the church with improvident rashness, in undertaking by themselves a work so important and so unusual, without consulting him, or making him a sharer in their proceedings.

"It was only fit," he said, "that he, seeing he was their neighbour, should have been called in as one who might afterwards state that he had been present at the investigation, and might, by his asseveration, stamp it with the impress of truth.

"It was probable enough," he said "that the brethren, as they had not permitted a member of any other church to witness their secret proceedings, were dealing in fiction rather than in fact. Reason," he added, "seems to require that the truth of such a marvellous thing should be investigated by others, that the people who have assembled in such numbers may be satisfied by the testimony of us, who, by ocular demonstration, have ascertained the fact."

These remarks he took care to make frequently in the hearing of those who had assembled, and there were some who began to think as he did upon the subject. The appointed day was already at hand, and the brethren having heard the calumnious remarks of the Abbot, were grievously scandalised that they themselves should be branded with the infamy of falsehood, and that a further exposure of the sacred body should be aimed at—a thing which they dared neither to permit to others, nor repeat themselves. There was, therefore, much vehemency on both sides. The Abbot insisted that the attestation of the brethren of the church ought not to be admitted with respect to their own deed; and the brethren, in confusion at the suspicion under which they laboured, exclaimed, that that man could only mediate either the ruin of their Monastery, or their own expulsion from it, who, repelling their testimony, even

when given upon oath, as false, held them up as sacrilegious and
worthy of detestation.

"Let it never be the case," said they, "that that man should have
an opportunity of seeing the sacred remains, through whose agency
we have fallen under the suspicion of a grievous falsehood. Even
some of those very men who yesterday sang along with us 'Glory
to God in the highest,' in glad strains of exultation, today, at the
instigation of this Abbot, hold us suspected of a lie."

The dispute is dramatic, like the ceremony itself, with parties playing
the roles of the cynic, the accused and the intermediary.

The contention was at its highest pitch, and no end seemed likely
to be put to it, when Ralph, then Abbot of Séez, but afterwards
Archbishop of Canterbury, a man of venerable memory, of much
mildness, and deeply read in the Holy Scriptures, stept forward as
a mediator between the parties.

"That is a true saying of Scripture," said he, "'in the mouth of
two or three witnesses shall every word be established,' but how
much more strongly ought it to be established in the mouth of a
numerous body of men, and those so worthy of credit, that reason
should permit no one to question their testimony. We believe that
a work of Divine power has been revealed in the body of Saint
Cuthbert; we believe, and for this my mouth speaks the praise of
the Lord, and my soul blesses his name. But seeing the evidence of
this miracle is so strong, perhaps I shall seem to be acting rashly, if
I should require the incorruption of the holy body manifested to
you, to be manifested to us also, and yet I ought to be considered
neither rash nor doing that which is unnecessary: but because
perfect charity casteth out fear, I presume, from my great affection,
to make a request, which I beg may be apologised for by charity.
It is no small furtherance to my prayer, that there is a doubt in
the mind of our brother Abbot, which, if it be not removed by the

testimony of others, as well as of you, will appear to have given rise to just complaints against you, and will make many entertain the same notion; for, in my opinion, this his slowness of belief proceeds from Divine Providence, that from that which you anticipate as the cause of grave offence, there should arise, by the dispensation of God, a still greater glory to this your church. For as soon as you have favourably attended to our request, and we ourselves have found that to be true, of which we had before only heard, the calumny of gainsayers will the sooner cease, in proportion as an experiment shall have corroborated your testimony and ours, and so much the more extensively will the glory of God in Saint Cuthbert be made known, as we, who have proved it with our eyes, as we return home in different directions, shall have set ourselves to divulge it to all the world."

The Bishop would at once have given his assent to the prayer of the venerable Abbot, had not the brethren conceived that his request ought not to be hastily complied with—fearing, as they did, some tremendous judgement from above, if they inadvisedly again exposed the holy body to view.

At length, influenced by the persuasion of their prudent friends, they very reluctantly agreed to this, that, putting aside the Abbot who had been of opinion that they were unworthy of belief, their humble and religious suitor, along with such others as might seem fit persons, should be admitted to a new inspection of the miracle. But, by the persuasion of their advisers, they at last admitted even the doubter himself—the man who, having been slow of belief himself, had shaken the belief of others; and they admitted him for this reason, that having seen the miracle with his own eyes, he might believe what he had refused to receive upon their authority.

The scene is now set for the final unscheduled act of the public ceremony: the revelation of what Symeon already knows is an incorrupt corpse.

The dispute having been thus arranged, the Prior led the way into the church, followed by the aforesaid Abbot of Séez; Richard, Abbot of St Alban's; Stephen, Abbot of St Mary at York; and Hugh, Abbot of St German at Ollesby [Selby], all clad in their albs; next came Alexander, brother of the King of Scotland, himself afterwards King, and William, then Chaplain to the Bishop of Durham, and afterwards Archbishop of Canterbury; then followed forty men, some of them monks, and the others secular clergy, but all of them devoted to a religious life; and these were succeeded by more brethren of the church—some were absent, but their services were required by the Bishop, who was at that very point of time dedicating an altar in the church.

After a prayer, devoutly uttered by all who were present, the sacred body was brought into the choir, and as soon as the coffin was opened by the brethren who had so lately closed it, the Prior raised his hand, and by a tremendous charge forbade any one, except the Abbot of Séez, from touching either the body or any thing connected with it. The rest he commanded to stand hard by, and make themselves acquainted with the truth by means of their eyes rather than their hands. Moreover, he charged the brethren of the monastery to pay unceasing attention to what was going on, and to watch with a vigilant eye, lest any one should by any means carry off even a particle of thread from the vestments in which the body was wrapped. His comments were obeyed.

The Abbot aforesaid, assisted by a brother of the church, having unfolded the vestments around the venerable head, raised it a little in both his hands, in the sight of all, and bending it backwards in different directions, found it perfect in all the joints of its neck, and firmly attached to the rest of the body. He next applied his hand to the ear, which he drew backwards and forwards in no gentle manner; and having proceeded to examine the other parts of the body with his inquisitive hand, found it consisting of solid nerves and bones, and clothed with the softness of flesh. Nay, holding it by the head, and shaking it as he held it, he so far raised it up that it seemed almost to assume a sitting posture in its quiet abode; and lest any thing should be overlooked in the diligent inquiry, he took care to ascertain the perfect state of its feet and legs.

The effect on the craning witnesses and on the waiting crowds would have been intense.

There were some who could no longer look upon such a scene as this with a fearless gaze, and covering their eyes with their hands, exclaimed, that he, the investigator, insisted upon a greater proof of the truth than circumstances called for, that he had before him the fact in all its certainty. After a while, when the inquisitor had over and above satisfied himself of the truth of the miracle, he raised his voice in the midst of the assembled multitude, and cried aloud, "My brethren, the body which we have before us is unquestionably dead, but it is just as sound and entire as when it was forsaken by its holy soul on its way to the skies."

After this, all things being arranged about the holy body as they had been before, those who were present pronounced the brethren of the monastery veracious and worthy to be trusted, and he who had a while before judged them unworthy of credit, affirmed, whether he would or not, in conjunction with the rest, that what he had before denied deserved to be believed.

They all straightway chanted the *Te Deum* in solemn exultation, and every thing which was necessary being decently arranged, the holy body of the Father was placed upon the shoulders of a fit number of bearers; and in honour of the Omnipotent God a band of singers scattered their celestial peals on the gale. The various caskets of relics, the remains of the other saints, went before—the venerable body of the blessed Cuthbert the Bishop followed after, and no sooner was it out of the door and in the open air, than the immense crowd which was waiting for it, from very joy, burst into tears, and fell flat on the ground, rendering it almost impossible for the procession to advance—all the while the voices of the singers were drowned by the strong cries of the praying, the exulting, and the weeping for joy.

Having gone round the outside of the new church, the procession halted at its eastern end, where the Bishop began a sermon, and there stood by his side men to inform the assembled multitudes of the fact that they had seen and handled this miracle of incorruption, which had lasted for four hundred and eighteen years. It was a matter of new exultation to them, that their devotion had been thought worthy to be rewarded with such a manifestation of celestial grace.

That day had far advanced, and the Bishop kept preaching on, touching many points not at all appropriate to the solemnity, and fairly wearing out the patience of many of his hearers by the prolixity of his discourse. The brightness of the day had been such that there was no sign of bad weather whatever in the sky, when on a sudden such torrents of rain began to fall, that the brethren, interrupting the sermon, snatched up the coffin in which the holy body was contained, and hastily conveyed it into the church.

No sooner had they done this than the rain straightway ceased; and the inference from this is plain, that it was not pleasing to God that the sacred body of his servant should be any longer detained in unholy ground. There is also another fact worthy to be recorded—that, notwithstanding the immense fall of rain, neither the ornaments of the church, which were all of them exposed to it, nor the robes of those who were dressed more splendidly than usual, received any injury whatever.

At length, the body having been decently restored to its place, a solemn mass was performed, whilst all the while the church was echoing with peals of praise, and the mysteries for the safety of the faithful being duly gone through, all returned home with joy, glorifying and praising God for what they have seen and heard.

CHAPTER FIVE

The Dissolution of the Monasteries

December 1539 (852 years and eight months after Cuthbert's death)

Why would you not go to Durham? In a world that made no sense, why would you not have gone to place your fragile self or hold your sick child near such power?

As you drew near the City from the south, the first things you would have seen were the towers: a rearing, breath-taking presence, like standing stones looming on the far horizon.

But that would have been lost in the realisation that you were getting closer; that the moment was near. For beneath the towers, behind the daunting castle walls hanging like a cliff face over the shanty buildings of the outer town, and on the hill beyond the looping moat made by the oxbow gorge of the river, there lay the thing you had come for: a singularity of spiritual power. For you knew that the towers on the horizon marked the position of the body of a man who had died hundreds of years before, but which looked and felt as fresh as the day it had been buried.

Yet this was not a source of horror and fascination, but of hope, and sometimes joy.

From first sighting the towers, you would have found yourself approaching the corpse through a series of encasements. First, you progressed around the glittering, encircling loop of water to the narrow northern opening to the peninsular on which the Cathedral lay. Then, turning south to head up the hill to the shrine, you would have faced into the sun and entered the shadow of the gates and castle walls that sealed the peninsular from the land outside. And with each gate passed, as each encasement opened, the pitch of yearning would have increased, until, as security gave way to reverence, you joined a slowly surging queue in the narrow streets and felt a quickening of suspense as you entered the Church itself. Its great, colour-filled space, the smoke, the chanting, the echoing shuffle of feet, the presence of a thousand other souls, both living and the dead: it was an atmosphere that could hush even a lively child. And then too soon, in a nervous rush, the moment of kneeling at the shrine, at one of the four alcoves around the shrine, the body itself a few inches from you in its final encasements, within its coffins, within the shrine cover. After all that anticipation, it was disorientatingly brief, too brief.

In this way, over hundreds of years the Norman monastery grew rich and the shrine more lavish. We know what it looked like because a rambling lament for what had once been was published in 1593, after the dissolution of the monastery. Titled *A Description or Brief Declaration of all the Ancient Monuments, Rites and Customs Belonging or Being Within the Monastical Church of Durham before the Suppression*, and known as *The Rites of Durham*, it was probably written by George Bates, the last Registrar of Durham before the dissolution and the Clerk of the Feretory (a receptacle to hold the relics of saints). This is what he says:

> His sacred shrine was exalted with most curious workmanship of fine and costly green marble, all lined and gilted in gold, having four seats or places convenient under the shrine for the pilgrims, lame or sick men sitting on their knees to lean and rest on, in time of their devout offerings and fervent prayers to God and holy Saint Cuthbert for his miraculous relief and succour, which being never wanting made the shrine to be so richly invested that it was estimated to be one of the most sumptuous monuments in all England; so great were the offerings and jewels that were bestowed upon it, and no less the miracles that were done by it even in these latter days, as is more apparent in the history of the Church at large.[11]

On Cuthbert's feast day—20 March, the anniversary of his death and of the first discovery of his corpse—the monks would ceremonially raise the shrine cover, an ornate lid with sides that extended over the coffin and hid it from view. As it was lifted, six silver bells attached to the ropes would make "such a good sound that it did stir all the people's hearts that were within the church to repair unto it, and to make their prayers to God and holy Saint Cuthbert, and that the beholders might see the glorious ornaments thereof."

[The] cover was all gilded over, and of either side was painted four lively images curious to the beholders; and on the east end was painted the picture of our Saviour sitting on a rainbow to give judgement, very lively to the beholders; and on the west end of it was the picture of our Lady and our Saviour on her knee. And on the top of the cover from end to end is most fine carved work, cut out with dragons and other beasts, most artificially wrought, and the inside was varnished with a fine sanguine colour that it might be more perspicuous to the beholders; and at every corner of the cover was a lock to keep it close, but at such times as was fit to show it, that the beholders might see the glory and ornaments thereof.

During the same ceremonies, the monks would throw open the "almeryes", the cupboards surrounding the shrine.

And within the said almeryes did lie all the holy relics and gifts that were offered to that holy man Saint Cuthbert. And when his shrine was drawn up then the said almeryes were opened, that every man that came thither at that time might see all the holy relics therein so that for the costly relics and jewels that was in the same almeryes, and other relics that hung about within the said feretory upon the irons, was accounted to be the most sumptuous and richest jewels in all this land, with the beautifulness of the fine little images that did stand in the French pier within the Feretory, for great was the

gifts and godly devotion of kings and queens and other estates at
this time towards God and holy Saint Cuthbert in this Church.

And, just as at Lindisfarne in 793, the wealth and vulnerability of
this and other monasteries eventually attracted raiders. This time,
however, the vulnerability was intellectual. Educated men and women
did not necessarily believe any more in miracle-working, divine
portals accessed through an incorrupt corpse. And with the legal
right and state power of an avaricious, disgruntled, lustful and clever
king behind them, they did not need an army to pillage the shrine,
cast out the monks, and trample the holy relics into the ground.

At Durham, it only took three officials, a goldsmith and a valuer
to end the devotion of 850 years.

This was one of the officials, Thomas Leigh, exulting about the
reception he received on his first, preliminary examination of the
Cathedral's wealth: "It would be too long to tell you the gentle and
lowly entertainment of the bishop of Durham," he wrote, "meeting us
at our entry into his diocese three or four miles from his house with
a great company of his servants, and on our leaving him conduct us
from Auckland more than half way to Durham Abbey."[12]

Thomas Leigh was an old Etonian, a University of Cambridge
lawyer and a former ambassador to Denmark, and this was what
he wanted: to be met with ceremony by the people whose way of
life he had come to destroy.

According to a colleague who went with him on a different
valuation, what Leigh liked was to be met with obsequious respect.
"Whenever he comes he handles the fathers very roughly," wrote the
shocked official, "many times for small causes, as for not meeting
him at the door, where they had been warned of his coming."[13]

He was not popular. There are reports from his colleagues to
the King's chief minister, Thomas Cromwell, telling tales of Leigh's
taking his brother along at the Crown's expense, of his insolence
and pompousness, and of his "notable sensualities".

Leigh defended himself to Cromwell in his own letters. "Though I was discomforted I was more surprised who should incense you against me. I pray I may not live to that day when I shall give any cause for deceiving your expectation of me. I shall always act as if you were present . . . sycophants would be glad to bring me out of your favour, though I have used no rigour at any time or place . . . and though a man is given to sensual appetites I am not addicted to such and abuses as you are informed."[14]

This then was the manner of man who, with two colleagues, Dr Henley and Mr Blytham, came to destroy the shrine in Durham and strip it of its value. It seems to have taken place in December 1539, and this is George Bates' account of what happened:

The sacred shrine of holy Saint Cuthbert, before mentioned, was defaced in the visitation that Dr Leigh, Dr Henley and Master Blytham, held at Durham for the subverting of such monuments, in the time of King Henry the Eighth, in his suppression of the abbeys, where they found many worthy and goodly jewels, but especially one precious stone, which by the estimate of those three visitors and their skilful lapidaries was of value sufficient to redeem a prince.

After the spoil of his ornaments and jewels, coming nearer to his body, thinking to have found nothing but dust and bones, and finding the chest that he did lie in, very strongly bound with iron, then the goldsmith did take a great forehammer of a smith, and did break the said chest, and, when they had opened the chest, they found him lying whole, incorrupt, with his face bare, and his beard as yet had been a fortnight's growth, and with all his vestments upon him, as he was accustomed to say mass withal, and his metwande of gold lying beside him.

Then, when the goldsmith did perceive that he had broken one of his legs, when he did break open the chest, he was very sorry for it and did cry "Alas I have broken one of his legs."

Dr Henley, hearing him say so, did call upon him, and did bid him cast down his bones.

He made him answer again that he could not get it in sunder, for the sinews and the skin held it, that it would not come in sunder.

Then Dr Leigh did step up, to see if it were so or not, and did turn himself about, and did speak Latin to Dr Henley that he was lying whole.

Yet Dr Henley would give no credit to his word, but still did cry "Cast down his bones."

Dr Leigh made answer "If you do not believe me, come up yourself and see him."

Then did Dr Henley step up to him, and did handle him, and did see that he laid whole. Then he did command them to take him down, and so it happened, contrary their expectation, that not only his body was whole and incorrupted, but the vestments, wherein his body lay, and wherewithal he was accustomed to say mass, was fresh, safe and not consumed.

Whereupon the visitors commanded that he should be carried to the Revestry, where he was close and safely kept, in the inner part of the Revestry, till such time as they did further know the King's pleasure, what to do with him . . . [15]

There is also a second account, by Nicholas Harpsfield, a Roman Catholic priest, writer and himself an active prosecutor of protestant believers during the reign of Queen Mary.

When, at the order of King Henry VIII, the shrines of the Saints were plundered and broken to pieces in every part of England, and their holy relics were cast into vile places, the wooden chest, which was covered with white marble, was also broken. And when he whose task it was to destroy and break the tomb, had broken the coffin with a heavy blow, the stroke fell upon the body of the Saint itself, and wounded the leg, and of the wound the flesh soon gave a manifest sign. As soon as this was seen, as also that the whole body was entire, except that the tip of the nose, I know not why, was wanting . . . Not only the body, but also the vestments in which he was robed, were perfectly entire, and free and clear of all stain and decay. He had on his finger a gold ring, ornamented with a sapphire, which I once saw and touched, and which, as a holy relic more precious than any treasure, I earnestly laid hold of and kissed. When this holy body was brought out and exposed, there were present, amongst others, Dr. Whithead, the head of the monastery, Dr. Sparke, Dr. Tod, and William Wilam, the keeper of the holy shrine. And thus it is abundantly evident that the body of Saint Cuthbert remained inviolate and incorrupt for 840 years.[16]

Although it is difficult to believe that the corpse still retained some bodily integrity after so many centuries, it is not impossible, and there are two circumstances that corroborate the accounts of the dispossessed: that the thing they believed was more or less true.

First, Leigh, Henry and Blytham seem to have stopped their investigation of the contents of the coffin at the point that George Bates described. They did not take the silver altar, the ring, or the golden-garnet cross, with its cloisonné infill the red of drying blood and its design like the book plates used at Aelfflaed's abbey. Perhaps the monks had hidden them away. And, instead of burning the corpse or throwing its bones onto a midden, as had happened elsewhere, Cromwell's men did not destroy what was left. Perhaps the consternation that George Bates ascribes to them was real, and these three unsentimental men were spooked by what they found.

But still no one knew what to do with the corpse. It lay in the Revestry for two years. It had not lain out like this since 1104, when it had been placed upon a tapestry on the pavement of the new Cathedral, and Symeon had kissed its feet in the torchlight and moistened them with his tears. And if George Bates and Nicholas Harpsfield were right, and the corpse was still whole when the goldsmith's forehammer crashed through the oak and hides of the travelling chest, through the carving of the animal symbols of the four Gospel writers on the lid of the Anglo-Saxon coffin-reliquary, and onto the leg of the Saint—if the body was still whole, it is difficult to believe that two years in the open air of the Revestry did not induce catastrophic deterioration. And we can imagine what symbolic presence those rags and bones in their broken coffin must have exerted on the minds of everyone in Durham as the religion of England changed. It must have been the ghost at every feast.

Then, after two years, they dug a grave beneath the former shine. We know this because the bill for the workmen still exists.[17] And, for the first time since 698, the corpse was buried beneath the ground.

This act, and the religious policy that supported it, did not only end the guardianship of a community of monks that in both Anglo-Saxon and Norman forms had been with Cuthbert since he first joined the order. It also destroyed the idea of the miraculous incorrupt corpse. The pilgrim's experience of ritually unwrapping the layers of encasement—the passing through gates, the entering of the Cathedral, the sighting of the shrine, the raising of the cover, the rare opening of the coffin—all this had likewise been destroyed. A raised shrine had become a deep grave, a place of decomposition. And the journey of the corpse had come full circle: from grave to shrine to roving gestalt lord to shrine to grave once more.

"And upon notice of the King's pleasure therein," wrote George Bates, "the Prior and Monks buried him, in the ground, under a fair marble stone which remains to this day, where his Shrine was exalted."

CHAPTER SIX

The Second Protestant Desecration

*17 May 1827 (1,140 years, one month and
27 days after Cuthbert's death)*

In 1827, a new Roman Catholic church was built in Durham, the first of its kind since the establishment of a separate Church of England in the middle of the sixteenth century. Although architecturally modest and discrete, the church's location in the shadow of the Cathedral excited some local protestant opinion. The controversy prompted the Cathedral librarian, the Reverend James Raine, to take it upon himself to demonstrate that the incorrupt corpse had always been a myth. In a gleeful orgy of rationalism and puerile enthusiasm, he broke open the grave and subjected its contents to a sceptical examination.

This is how John Lingard, a local Roman Catholic writer, responded to the news of Raine's investigation.

On the 17th May, 1827, "the Reverend Williams Nicholas Darnell, B.D. prebendary of the sixth stall in the cathedral of Durham, the Reverend Stephen Gilly, M.A. prebendary of the ninth stall, and the Reverend James Raine, M.A. and rector of Meldon, attended by the deputy receiver, the clerk of the works, the verger and the master mason," repaired to that part of the Abbey church, which is called the feretory of Saint Cuthbert. There they removed a stone slab from the pavement, opened the ground, and taking out the skeleton of a human being, subjected its bones to a long and minute examination.

The reader will naturally ask, what could have led to this extraordinary, this unseemly proceeding. It was, (the Reverend gentlemen avowed it,) a charitable desire on their part to open the eyes of the blind deluded papists to the impostures of their church, by demonstrating to them that the body of the patron saint, in defiance of its boasted incorruptibility, is crumbled into dust. How ingenious is the zeal of proselytism! How easily does it accommodate itself to the wants and prejudices of its objects! In Ireland the second reformation began with the exhibition of good cheer to the poor and the hungry; in Durham it begins in a much more solemn manner. It disturbs the repose of the dead, and profanes the sanctity of the grave.

It would appear that these Reverend gentlemen are but little acquainted with the state of the catholic mind in this country. To the generality of Catholics the name of Saint Cuthbert is scarcely known beyond the limits of the bishopric; and neither there nor elsewhere is it believed, that the truth or falsehood of their creed has any connexion with the truth or falsehood of the the legend respecting Saint Cuthbert's body. Many, indeed, among them are persuaded that there is sufficient historic proof of that body having for ages been preserved without decay. But this notion is not peculiar to them. The same has obtained among eminent protestant divines. "This," says Wharton, "is most certain, that his body remained incorrupt for many ages after its burial." But with both, Catholics as well as Protestants, this was matter merely of historic opinion. Neither the one nor the other were such illogical reasoners as to conclude that, if the body were once incorrupt, it must of necessity remains so still, or that, if by the miraculous interposition of Providence it was preserved in the past ages, the same miraculous interposition must be perpetuated down to the present time.

Under the notion, however, that Catholics are taught to believe in the incorruptibility of Saint Cuthbert's body, the Reverend gentlemen resolved to investigate on the 17th of May, the contents of his reputed grave; and to Mr Raine has been allotted the distinguished honour of recording, for the instruction of the present and of future generations, the proceedings of that most memorable day. This task he has executed in a goodly volume of the quarto size, and of almost 500 closely printed pages, entitled "Saint Cuthbert, with an account of the state in which his remains were found, etc." For the antiquarian lore, with which his work is enriched, he deserves the thanks of his readers. But this is all. He possesses not that cool dispassionate judgement, which his task required. He writes evidently under the full influence of religious prejudice . . . and betraying in almost every page the most feverish anxiety to discover, or excogitate, proofs of fraud against the ancient clergy of Durham.[18]

This is what Raine found, in his own words.

I now come to St Cuthbert in the year 1827 (Thursday, May 17), eleven hundred and forty-two years from his becoming Bishop of Lindisfarne; eleven hundred and thirty-nine years from his death; eleven hundred and twenty-eight years from the reported discovery of his body in a state of incorruption; nine hundred and fifty-two years from the final removal of his bones and See from Lindisfarne; nine hundred and forty-four years from the establishment of the Cathedral at Chester-le-Street; eight hundred and thirty-two years from its removal to Durham; seven hundred and twenty-three years from the Translation of the remains of the Saint into the Shrine devoted to his name; and two hundred and eighty-five years from the ultimate burial of those remains in the ground beneath that part of the pavement upon which they had rested in their exalted state.

On the 17 May, 1827, in the presence of the Reverend William Nicholas Darnell, B. D., Prebendary of the sixth Stall, and in the above year Sub-Dean; the Rev. William Stephen Gilly, M. A.,

Prebendary of the ninth Stall, and at the time the Prebendary in residence; Mr John Leybourne, Deputy Receiver; Mr. Edward Fairclough, Clericus Operum; Mr. Anthony Tyler, Verger; Mr. Williams Joplin, Master Mason; and of the writer of these pages, as the first step towards the contemplated investigation, the above stone, placed over the grave in 1542, and spoken of in 1655, measuring eight feet ten inches and three quarters in length, and four feet three inches and three quarters in breadth, of Frosterly marble, was with some difficulty removed from its place. Its thickness was proportionate to its length and breadth, and, as has been already stated, its surface was perfectly smooth, and uninscribed. The removal of this slab did not, as might have been expected, at once expose to view the coffin and grave of the Saint. Nothing appeared, save a level surface of soil, which, however, upon investigation, was found to be only about eighteen or twenty inches in thickness, and to rest upon another large grey stone of a size almost equal to the one above-mentioned. The upper surface of this latter slab was in a rough and unfinished state, but upon being raised from its place this circumstance was easily accounted for. It was, in fact, in an inverted position, and, on its smooth lower side, there was, in the neatly carved black letter in use in the early part of the fifteenth century, the inscription, "*Ricardus heswell monarchus*".

This slab, upon its removal, disclosed to view a stone grave, if I may so call it, in the shape of a parallelogram, about seven feet in length, four in width, and from four to five in depth, the sides and ends of which were built not with brick, but with freestone, the masonry of which was finished in a very workmanlike manner, and, in consequence of the exclusion of the air, perfectly white and fresh.

The removal of the slab meant that Raine and his companions were the first people to see St Cuthbert's coffin in over 250 years.

But to return: at the bottom of the grave, extending nearly from one end to another, and almost from side to side, there appeared a large high coffin of oak in great decay, not shaped after the usual manner, (I mean with projecting shoulders,) but in the form of a parallelogram, and of that dusky colour which oak always assumes after a long period of years. The state and condition of this outer coffin may be easily described. Its lid was nearly entire, but probably from having been made of green timber, or from the influence of the damp masonry by which it had been originally surrounded, it had completely detached itself from the coffin on end and side; and to use a term, for which I have to thank Mr Fairclough, it was dished upwards, both in length and breadth, like a scroll of parchment shrivelled before the fire: and at first sight it might have been taken for a trough, which it closely resembled. The mouldings of the lid and sides, notwithstanding their thickness, were all loose and broken into short disjointed pieces; the ends and sides were in the same state; and, that the nature of the wood was completely exhausted, was evident from its light and brittle state.

The fragments of this outer coffin were gradually removed, when another coffin was discovered, but in a still more decayed condition. Enough of it, however, remained, to prove that it had been plain, and made of oak an inch in thickness; and there were here and there clinging to it portions of an envelope, which, whatever it might have originally been, had, from length of time, settled into a white adhesive substance, of which there were numerous and distinct traces. That this covering had not been of linen was manifest, for linen, however decayed, would have been traceable by its threads. I have no hesitation in considering this as the very coffin mentioned above in 1104, as the second coffin of the Saint, and at that time covered with skins. I have already said that this coffin was in a state of very great decay; but it was especially so as to its lid. This fact prevents me from distinctly localizing another discovery, made at the very time when this second coffin was first observed, I mean a large collection of human bones, loosely huddled together towards the lower end of the chest. I know not whether the proper place of these relics was upon or beneath the lid of this second coffin, as they were so confounded with its fragments; but it is of little consequence, seeing they had no connection with the Saint himself. These relics consisted of a skull and several ribs, arms, thighs, and legs, of a full-grown size; and besides these, there was the skull of a child, and numerous rib bones of other infants. These latter, and the bones above mentioned, all lay in a confused state at the lower end of the coffin. The former I believe to have been the relics, in particular, of the early Bishops of Lindisfarne, which were removed from thence along with the remains of Saint Cuthbert in 875, were taken from his coffin in 1104, and were, till the Dissolution, preserved in his shrine.

"I must admit," says Raine, "that this part of the investigation was very hastily gone through, from an over anxiety to reach at once the real object of our curiosity", and his haste and attitude contrasts with the awed reverence that the Norman monks showed on making the same discovery.

The above relics, which were numerous, were speedily removed; and during the process, the lid of a third coffin was discovered below them, but in such a state of decay, that portions of it were almost necessarily raised along with the superincumbent bones and fragments of wood. During this part of the investigation, an iron ring was found, which I shall notice by and by; and there was also raised from the lower end of the grave another full-grown skull, in a somewhat imperfect state, the resting-place of which was evidently beneath the last-mentioned lid. That this was the reputed skull of King Oswald, which the anonymous Monk and Reginald both prove to have been the only relic replaced in the coffin of Saint Cuthbert in 1104, may fairly be presumed. The situation in which it was found fully admits of the supposition. Perhaps under all the circumstances of the case, with such a discovery, and such historical information upon the point, before me, I may be blamed for conjecturing.

Raine has now reached the third coffin, the original Anglo-Saxon reliquary prepared by the carpenters on Lindisfarne in 698 and almost certainly not seen since Symeon's investigation of 1104.

This also was of oak, in general about three quarters of an inch in thickness, although in places much thinner, and of the same shape as the two already described. Its lid and sides were, from extreme old age, collapsed and much broken; and "the touch of time" had so completely exhausted the nature of its wood, that a portion, measuring about ten inches in length, and nine in breadth, weighs only thirteen ounces. Besides, there were fragments curled up, if I may so say, after the manner of the lid of the outer coffin, above described. The structure of this coffin appears to have been simple. The sketch of its joint, in the margin, of the full size, will easily be understood; and I have only to add, that along that part of the grooved receptacle, marked, there ran two or three thickly intertwisted threads of woollen, to exclude the air, many portions of which were remaining.

Notwithstanding the decayed state of this third and last coffin, enough remained to prove that it was the very coffin described by Reginald, and the anonymous Monk; and further, upon their testimony the identical coffin in which the remains of Saint Cuthbert were placed in the year 698, eleven years after his death.

According to the Monk, when the inner coffin of Saint Cuthbert was exposed to view in 1104, it was found to be enveloped in a covering of coarse cloth of a triple texture, which was removed in order to facilitate the then meditated investigation, and after that investigation it was again covered with "linen cloth of a coarse texture dipped in wax". Now, pieces of cloth of this very nature, coarse and strong, some of them almost an inch in breadth, were found closely adhering to divers fragments of the coffin which I am describing.

But to proceed:—The Monk informs us, that the lid of Saint Cuthbert's coffin in 1104, was raisable by means of two iron rings, one at the head and the other at the feet; and Reginald, after stating the same fact in still more minute terms, adds that there was no lock or fastening by which the lid was attachable to the coffin. Now in our late investigation these statements were proved to be perfectly correct. The lid had evidently been always loose, and moreover, in proof of their assertion as to the rings, a ring was at the same time discovered, 4¼ inches broad, so perfectly different from those above described, and of a shape so apparently calculated for a horizontal surface upon which it was intended to lie flat when not in use, that I have no hesitation in considering it as one of the two rings in question. The other ring was overlooked amid the mass of broken wood and bones above-mentioned. As a further proof of the fact with respect to the rings, the lower part of the iron loop by which one of them was held, is still remaining in a portion of the lid.

Again, Reginald states, that the whole of the inner coffin of Saint Cuthbert was ascertained in 1104 to be externally carved with very admirable engravings, of minute and most delicate workmanship; that in small and circumscribed tracts or compartments, there were "beasts, flowers, and images" or figures, "engrafted, engraved, or furrowed in the wood".

Now, listen to a description of the ornamental part of the inner coffin of Saint Cuthbert in 1827, as far as its fragments can be described.

The external surface of its lid, ends, sides and bottom, were occupied by various engravings; the upper part of one of which I have given at full size; and my reader, from the following description, with that plate before him, will fully comprehend the workmanship, if I may so call it, of these most ancient specimens of Saxon art. Their execution is the same wherever they occur, and it is quite interesting to observe how accurately Reginald must have been informed as to this part of his statement. Any one of the verbs which he uses in his description would have amply served his purpose; but the three are beyond measure descriptive. The carvings, one and all, with all their accompaniments, appeared to have been partly cut upon the surface of the wood by a sharp-pointed knife or chisel, and partly by some such instrument as the scrieve of the woodman; and in confirmation of Reginald's statement, that there were subdivisions or tracts, a slight single line, made with the point of a knife, but now scarcely discernible, runs between each engraving.

Now, Raine reaches the object of his scepticism: the corpse itself.

After the larger fragments of the lid, sides, and ends of the coffin, which I have last described, were removed from the grave, there appeared at its bottom a dark substance, of the length of a human body, which, after a moment's investigation, proved to be a skeleton, lying with its feet to the east, swathed apparently in one or more shrouds of linen or silk, through which there projected, in their respective places, the brow of the skull, and the lower part of the leg bones. The bones of the feet were disjointed and fallen flat. In this stage of the process, it was deemed advisable to elevate the whole substance from the bottom of the grave before any further examination was made; and for this purpose one strong board was placed longitudinally, and three transversely, under the lowest bottom of the coffin, by means of which the remains were raised up in an undisturbed state, and placed upon trestles on the spot—a step which most materially facilitated the subsequent investigation. Here it should be remarked, that the bottom of the grave was perfectly dry, and free from any offensive smell; nor was there any, even the slightest, symptom that a human body had ever undergone decomposition within its walls. The same remark must be made with respect to the body itself. The only unpleasant smell connected with it, arose from the mouldy and somewhat damp state of the robes in which it was swathed.

But before describing the skeleton, Raine with an apparently calm meticulousness sets himself to recording the various vestments and silks in which the corpse was swathed.

Our first step, after the skeleton was raised out of its grave, was to free it still more carefully from the broken wood and dust which rested upon it; and in doing this, it was impossible to leave uninjured the robes by which it was protected: some of them were, in fact, in such a state of decay, as scarcely to endure the slightest touch.

The first or outer envelope had evidently been of linen: but it must be admitted, that of this only a few small portions were observable, and these much discoloured by time ... Now, the Monk and Reginald both state, that in 1104 the body, after all its other swathements, was wrapped up in a linen winding-sheet of this nature, as its outermost covering.

The robes beneath this winding-sheet were still more decayed: so much so, in fact, that it was quite impossible to detach them one by one, or to preserve any accurate account of their respective shapes, or the order in which they occurred.

I have before me fragments of at least five, all of silk: and although some of them were unquestionably above, and some below the stole, and the other more perfect relics hereafter mentioned, I prefer giving a description of them at once, and shall afterwards try to assign to them their respective places upon the body, from Reginald's description.

1. A robe of thinnish silk ... The ground colour of the whole is amber; and the ornamental parts were literally covered with leaf gold, of which there remained distinct and very numerous portions.

It is interesting to observe the curious combination of ornaments upon this robe. The knight himself, and his horse dressed in the Saxon fashion, and equipped with hawk and hound, for fowl or four-footed beast, is a natural embellishment—but then there is the "flagrans telum" [thunderbolt] of Jove, and still lower down a border of rabbits "dancing it trippingly" above the fringe, which fringe is a braid of the same colour stitched on with a needle. The knight might be an appropriate ornament for the period, the thunder-bolt might be a trace of heathenism then fast wearing away; but I am of opinion, that the ornament of the rabbit had a special reference to Saint Cuthbert, and to Lindisfarne, the scene of his exaltation, which must always have abounded with this timid animal.

2. A robe of thick soft silk. A line stretching from side to side of the outermost circle of the pattern . . . The ground work or lower part of the circle is evidently the sea, in which six porpoises and four eider ducks are taking their pastime; above these, however strange, there stands within the circle, upon the surface of the waves, an urn, or some such receptacle, filled with fruit and flowers, but it is to be regretted that the outline of the upper part of this ornament could not be obtained. The inner part of the circular border is occupied exclusively by a succession of grapes and pears, or a similar fruit; and in the space left between one circle and another, stands another basket of fruit and flowers, with a solan goose on each side, of the same size as the annexed . . . The colours of this robe have once been brilliant beyond measure, but they are now much faded. The ground within the circle is red, the urn or flower basket, the eider ducks, and the sea, red, yellow, and purple; the porpoises yellow and red; the ground of the border is purple tinted with red; the fruit and foliage yellow with red stalks; and the pattern which runs round the border, red . . .

3. Of silk,—the ground amber . . . Around this robe, judging from the portions of it which were preserved, there was a border of thick lace . . . evidently owing its origin, not to the needle, but

to the loom, and of a pattern much resembling the coach lace of
the present day . . .

4. Of silk. Colours purple and crimson; the only prominent
ornament a cross—often repeated, even upon the small portion
which remains.

5. Of silk. A rich damask pattern in ovals . . . An urn stood
in the centre of the oval, supported by griffins. The colours were
crimson and purple . . .

With the same apparent patience, Raine takes his reader though the
other material relics that were found in the coffin.

The comb . . . was found . . . among the folds of one of the very
uppermost robes of the Saint, upon the lower part of the breast; but
in so frangible a state, that the slightest touch broke away the part
of which it attempted to lay hold . . . but every one who saw the
fragments, as they were removed one after another, pronounced the
comb to have been made of box-wood, or some such material. This
conclusion was formed from its red tinge, and from its breaking
asunder in parallel lines like wood. Its component parts, however,
were carefully collected, and afterwards still more carefully put
together by Mr Matthew Thompson, so as in every respect to
warrant the engraving; and during the process, the tediousness of
which may be easily ascertained from the lines which run through
its middle, for into so many parts was it broken, its material was
most clearly ascertained to be of ivory . . .

Near to the comb, but somewhat higher upon the breast of the
body, was found the silver altar, alluded to by the anonymous Monk,
afterwards mentioned by him by name, and last of all by Reginald
. . . The altar, although said to be of silver, was only so externally.
It consisted, in fact, of a square slip of oak, about a third of an inch
in thickness, totally covered on edge and side with a thin plate of
silver somewhat raised at the margin, and attached to it by nails

of the same material. Of this plate, the fragments were preserved, which constitute the square delineation on the upper part of my engraving; but they are so few, that I am quite at a loss to explain satisfactorily to myself, the imperfect inscription which runs in a circle round the cross in the centre . . . The reverse of the altar was equally covered with silver; but of this the remains were still more indistinct and imperfect . . . Between the silver lamina and the wood below, was a composition, apparently of paste, or some such material, of almost the eighth of an inch in thickness, which had evidently been in a soft state when the silver covering was first applied, as the parts of it which were perfect exhibited an accurate outline of the ornamental parts of the plate. This coating fell rapidly into dust; and no sooner was the wood, the ground-work of the whole, exposed to the air, than it also became so exceedingly brittle as not to bear handling . . .

We next observed, nearly in the same position, the burse, or small linen bag, for holding the sacramental elements.

Raine also found the remains of a stole and maniple, a kind of priestly scarf and handkerchief, and almost certainly the ones that were given to St Cuthbert during the visit of King Athelstan and his army in 934.

I now come to the stole, and maniple . . . I begin with the stole, which, although broken into five pieces, is in other respects perfect; and, as far as the gold in its fabric is concerned, as brilliant as the day it was made . . . it is no easy matter to convey to my reader a just idea of its fabric or colours. In the first place, the ground-work of the whole is woven exclusively with thread of gold: I do not mean by thread of gold, the silver-gilt wire frequently used in such matters, but real gold thread, if I may so term it, not round but flat . . . The figures are of tapestry work, and the prevalent colour of their drapery has been crimson, tinged deeply here and there with green; the more prominent parts of the folds are enlivened with threads of gold, of the same nature as those described above. The clouds, if they be intended for clouds, upon which the figures stand, have been tinged with crimson, blue, and green, in shades, and separated from each other by gold. The letters are occasionally red, but most frequently green; the inner ornamental parts of the nimbus a reddish scarlet and gold, and the foliage above the figures is of crimson, green, and purple. The border on each side is most evidently of needle work. The outer edge is a dark brown, approaching almost to black—next adjoining to this runs a line of scarlet, and after this the other divisions are scarlet and gold alternately; the scrawled ornament in the middle is scarlet, upon a ground of gold. . . . The maniple . . . the fabric, colours, and reverse, are precisely the same as those of the stole above described . . . I have already stated, that at each end of the maniple there hangs a fringe of crimson purple, an inch and three quarters in length . . .

A girdle and two bracelets of gold tissue were found upon the bones of Saint Cuthbert . . . It has evidently proceeded from the loom; and its two component parts are a flattish thread of pure gold, and a thread of scarlet silk, which are not combined in any particular pattern, save that at a very short distance from each selvage there run two or three longitudinal lines, which serve to break the uniformity of the whole. The lining is of silk. The bracelets are made of precisely the same materials and workmanship, only their border is checked, and saving that their scarlet threads are somewhat discoloured by time, they are as perfect as in the day they were made . . .

Finally, and without evidence of any excitement, Raine details the finding of the cross. He is the first person in history to mention it.

I next come to the cross . . . which was found deeply buried among the remains of the robes which were nearest to the breast of the Saint.

The cross is of gold—but the gold appears to have undergone some process, tending to deaden its lustre, for its dingy appearance can scarcely be the effect of time. There is a large garnet in the centre, one in each angle, and twelve upon each of its branches. The loop by which it has been suspended is of bright yellow gold, in its purest state. The arm which stands the lowest upon my engraving was found broken off; and upon examination, it appeared to have been broken once before, as there were evident proofs that it had been repaired by means of small rivets, some of which were remaining. The whole weighs fifteen pennyweights and twelve grains. Portions of the silken cord, twisted with gold, by which it had been suspended round the neck, were observed upon the breast of the skeleton . . .

We next observed divers fragments of the finest and most pliant gold wire, partly surrounding the skull, and partly entangled among the wrappers in which the skull had been enveloped. Judging from the position in which they were found, it appeared that they had originally been intended to bind fast the coif in which the head of the skeleton had been clad. One portion, in particular, had evidently encircled the skull, and its ends had as evidently been twisted together at their junction, to secure the something which it surrounded. It was a portion of this wire, which, about the year 1022, Elfred Westoue, the Sacrist, was in the habit of taking out of the coffin, and exhibiting as the hair of the Saint, defying the flames. Well might it glitter in the fire like gold, when it was gold indeed.

Raine had now reached the object of his enquiry, the corpse itself, and he is eager to confirm his protestant suspicion that the miracle of Cuthbert's incorrupt corpse was nothing but a fraud.

After this we proceeded to remove the wreck of a variety of robes, which had so far fallen in pieces, from extreme length of time, that few of their fragments were more than an inch in breadth. Still all was dry—at least, the only damp was that of mouldiness—and still there was no unpleasant smell. There were no traces whatever of a cerecloth, or any other preservative against corruption. There was nothing glutinous or fragrant; but every one who was present, was convinced that the bones had been thoroughly dry when originally clothed in their numerous habiliments.

My reader must now conceive, stretched at length before him, the skeleton of Saint Cuthbert; the bones of which, although disjointed and detached from each other, were yet all of them perfectly whole, and in their proper places, with the exception of the fingers and feet bones, which were in a state of confusion. The skeleton, when thus laid bare, measured five feet eight inches from the crown of the skull to the ankle joints, and we were enabled to ascertain very satisfactorily, that, saving its bones, the only other mouldering remains were those of silk or linen. There was not the slightest particle of soil, or any other trace of human flesh in a state of decomposition. The right arm was elevated in benediction . . .

The skull of the Saint was easily moved from its place; and when this was done, we observed on the forehead, and apparently constituting a part of the bone itself, a distinct tinge of gold, of the breadth of an ordinary fillet. Not a thread remained in connection with this appearance. Still the place which it occupied, and the direction which it took, left no doubt that it had been occasioned by something pressing hard upon the bone, in the composition of which gold had formed a part. Now, if my reader will refer to Reginald, he will there read, that in 1104 there was a fillet of gold, set with precious stones, observed upon the forehead of the Saint. No precious stones, however, came under our notice, nor any other trace of the bandage, save the yellow tint upon the skull—which, be it remembered, could never have become so imprinted if flesh and blood had at any time intervened between its cause and the bone. Again, Reginald states, that the whole of Cuthbert's head and face were, in the year 1104, found to be closely covered by a cloth, so carefully put on, that it appeared glued to the parts which it concealed, that no art could separate it from the skin and flesh to which it was attached; but that through it might be seen the nostrils and eye-lids. Now, we found adhering to the skull, pieces of the finest cloth, and so adhering to it, as most thoroughly to convince those who saw them, that the envelope, of which they formed a part, had been put upon the skull when that skull was nothing more than a bare dry bone. What would have become of so thin a coating of cloth, if the "hairy scalp" of the Saint had remained to fall away into corruption beneath it? And how, under such circumstances, could such distinct portions of that said thin grave-cap have remained in the place and condition in which they were found? But to return from inference to fact—Will it be believed?—the eye-holes of this said skull, in order to give to the above face-cloth the projecting appearance of eyes in their respective places, had been originally, and still continued, stuffed full with a whitish composition, which admirably retained its colour and consistency; and which, upon being removed from its place, was easily pressed into a powder by the finger and thumb.

I have now come to the naked skull of Saint Cuthbert . . . Let me proceed to compare the skull of Saint Cuthbert with Reginald's description of his face, as it was observed in 1104. By face, it must be understood, the bones of his face, as they were closely covered with the cloth above-mentioned. His nose, says my author, as its junction with his forehead, seemed to be turning somewhat rapidly outwards, and the tip of the lower bone of his chin appeared to be furrowed by a well-defined line of division, which in fact was so deep, that a finger might be almost laid in the cavity. Does not the skull given above exactly correspond with this description? There is the obcurve nose most distinctly marked, and there is the chin bone much more deeply indented than could well be delineated in the engraving. I subjoin the following further remarks upon this singular skull, made by a medical gentleman, who had a hasty opportunity of examining it, before Reginald had been consulted:

Forehead flat and prominent; ... space from the angle of the eye to the base of the skull, measuring over the frontal and occipital bones, unusually long; very narrow across the forehead; ... orbits deep; nasal bone short, and turned upwards in a very singular manner; upper jaw very prominent; the chin still more remarkably so; distance from top of frontal bone to the insertion of the teeth, remarkably short; eight teeth remaining in the upper jaw, and six in the lower, sound, and large; one of the canini, or eye teeth, of the upper jaw, peculiarly large, and projecting outwards; the skull, upon the whole, rather small.

We had now reached the bottoms of the various coffins above described; but these it was next to an impossibility to remove one by one; or even to note their number, or the order in which they occurred. Properly speaking, there should have been four; the false bottom placed in the inner coffin in 1104, the original bottom of that same coffin, and those of the two outer ones above described—and for all these there was apparently wood enough. The only point which could be ascertained was, that one bottom had been externally ornamented with carvings; but still this great decay had been caused solely by time: no trace of corruption was observable.

After those portions of the various coffin bottoms, which could be removed, had been laid aside, the whole accumulation of crumbled wood and robes was thoroughly examined, lest any thing should have escaped our notice. This was done by means of a sieve; but no further discovery was made.

Having proven their point to their own satisfaction, Raine and his companions decided what to keep out and what to leave in the grave. The skeleton and the other bones are returned to the tomb; the fragments of cloth and of the Anglo-Saxon coffin, together with the cross and comb and other cultural relics are retained in the

Cathedral. Other relics such as the burse and some of the textiles simply disappear from history, never to be seen again.

> The next step was to re-inter the bones of the Saint and the other relics which had been found along with him. For this purpose, a new coffin was prepared, in which they were one and all placed; and this coffin was, in the same evening, deposited in the bottom of the original grave, upon a mass of broken wood, iron rings, and iron bars, the remnants of the two outer coffins of the Saint, which had been thrown into the grave. Heswell's stone was again placed over the vault, the soil was re-laid, and the blue stone was again applied as a covering to the whole.
>
> Those portions of the inner coffin which could be preserved, including one of its rings, with the silver altar, cross, comb, stole, two maniples, bracelets, girdle, gold wire, the fragments of the five robes above described, and some of the rings of the outer coffin made in 1542, were not restored to the grave, but were deposited in the Library of the Dean and Chapter, where they are now preserved.[19]

On first reading, Raine's account seems to reveal a sensibility perfectly poised between antiquarianism, a protestant or enlightenment rationalism and a modern forensic archaeology. On subsequent readings, however, it begins to look more ramshackle.

"There were three of these rods on each side of the coffin," he writes at one point, "and perhaps one at each end, but of this I have no memorandum."

Then at another: "I know not whether the proper place of these relics was upon or beneath the lid of this second coffin . . . ; but it is of little consequence . . . "

And so on and on: "This part of the investigation was very hastily gone through, from an over anxiety to reach at once the real object of our curiosity."

"It was quite impossible to detach them one by one, or to preserve any accurate account of their respective shapes, or the order in which they occurred."

"It was next to an impossibility to remove one by one; or even to note their number, or the order in which they occurred."

"The new coffin was, in the same evening, deposited . . . upon a mass of broken wood, iron rings, and iron bars, the remnants of the two outer coffins of the Saint, which had been thrown into the grave."

Thrown into the grave.

The most likely interpretation for this near-desecration is that Raine had not had approval from his colleagues at the Cathedral. No discussion about the investigation is minuted in the Cathedral records,[20] and this makes his overblown list of the names, titles and qualifications of those present look like an an attempt at legitimisation (a reading that the Roman Catholic commentator Lingard seems to pick up on when he sarcastically repeats it in his anonymous commentary on the investigation).

There are other clues. For example, the Reverend William Nicholas Darnell, *B. D., Prebendary of the sixth Stall, and in the above year Sub-Dean* and the first of Raine's named collaborators, was not necessarily the willing colleague that Raine helps us to infer. In a letter written a couple of months later, Darnell berated him, presumably without irony, declaring "I wish no evil may befall you for having been engaged in this wicked spoliation of the dead."[21]

It is the same with the Reverend William Stephen Gilly, *M. A., Prebendary of the ninth Stall, and at the time the Prebendary in residence* and the second in Raine's list.

Fourteen years later, Gilly called on Lingard and gave him information that Lingard repeated in a letter he wrote to a friend the next day.

Yesterday Doctor Gilly, prebendary of Durham, called. He was according to the extract from Raine in the little book which I sent you one of the openers of Saint Cuthbert's tomb. He tells me that he was not: but hearing in the choir a strange noise in the feretory, the moment the service was over he ran there in his surplice to see what as going on, and there found Darnell and Raine with two workmen, the latter actually standing within the coffin and trampling on the contents. He ordered them out, remonstrated with Darnell and requested that witnesses might be sent for out of the town and someone from Ushaw [the nearby Roman Catholic college]. Darnell was sub-dean and seemed very nervous, but refused. He wished to finish the investigation as quickly as possible and to prevent and crown assembling. Gilly then went down himself and discovered two stoles and maniple, the altar of oak covered with silver, the gold cross on the breast and the paten lying by it[22]

According to the local paper, the investigation "occasioned a great sensation in the town,"[23] so it may be that despite the scholarly, forensic tone of Raine's account, the investigation itself was so chaotic, unauthorised and hurried because he feared a crowd might gather.

CHAPTER SEVEN

The Victorian Investigation

11.25 a.m., 1 March 1899 (1,211 years, eleven months and nine days after Cuthbert's death)

It was the puzzle of the Anglo-Saxon coffin-reliquary that made them open the grave again.

Most of the fragments had been scooped out of the grave by Raine, and by the late nineteenth century, an attempt was being made to recreate the work of the Lindisfarne carpenters by piecing together their carvings of the beardless Christ, the seven archangels, the twelve apostles, the four symbols of the gospel writers and the baby Jesus with his mother. It was now obvious that some of the pieces were missing and the suggestion was made that the tomb should be reopened so that more fragments could be found.

This time, however, it was to be an official investigation.

"After many delays," writes Canon J.T. Fowler, "caused by the strong feeling in the minds of some whose objections rightly carried great weight, it was decided that the grave should be opened, the coffin of 1542 carefully raised, the other contents of the grave taken out, and the coffin returned to its place with its contents undisturbed."[24]

Canon Fowler was a medical practitioner, a priest, a Durham University lecturer and librarian, and Vice-President of the Surtees Society—a scholarly local history organisation. Apart from his main account of the opening, there are two others. The first is a chapter in a series called *Victoria County History*[25] by George Kitchin, the Dean of the Cathedral and the first Chancellor of Durham University. The second comprises articles and letters-to-the-editor by Father William Brown who, with a modern sensitivity, was invited to observe as a

representative of the Roman Catholic faith. This is Canon Fowler's
introduction to what happened:

> Our Fellow and Local Secretary, Canon Greenwell, has recently
> devoted much time, thought, and labour to the piecing together of
> the broken portions of Saint Cuthbert's coffin that were removed
> from the grave in 1827. Special attention having thus been directed
> to the matter, it was thought desirable that another examination
> of the grave should be made in order to recover, if possible, some
> of the missing fragments.

Work was set to begin on the morning of Wednesday 1 March 1899,
and Father Brown got there just in time to see what lay beneath the
blue marble slab that marked the site of both the former shrine and
the grave. He writes:

> [The workman] made an early start so that when I reached the
> Feretory about eleven a.m., the ponderous "blues stone" that
> indicates the position of the ancient shrine of Saint Cuthbert, had
> already been lifted from its bed ... A smooth surface of brown
> sand and pebbles, apparently brought up from the river, then
> lay exposed to view. The layer, for such it proved to be, was dealt
> with most carefully, and it was all passed through a riddle. At the
> outset, in a basin-shaped hole, immediately beneath the surface, a
> bundle of decayed paper was found, containing a quantity of fringe
> material, over looked, no doubt, until the last moment in the hasty
> 1827 search, and huddled away there just before the "blue stone"
> was replaced. The threads of the fringe were pink but covered with
> gilt. Among the sand and gravel were found pieces of rusty iron,
> small fragments of the coffins, fragments of bone and a tooth.[26]

This was yet more evidence that Raine had been in a careless hurry,
but it would not be the last. When the investigators were able to look

down into the grave, what they saw shocked them. This is Father Brown's recollection:

> I had expected to gaze upon a substantial arca [coffin] standing clear of the debris whereon it rested, and I felt correspondingly puzzled, when instead a dark confused mass was seen lying at the bottom of the grave. When a lantern had been lowered, three narrow pieces of wood, discoloured with damp were observed upon the surface separated from each other by an inch or so of space. Their appearance suggested the top of a crate, or a rough packing-case.
>
> Believing them to be some sort of covering to the "new coffin", provided in 1827, a workman, from the steps of a short ladder, essayed to raise them; but they not only broke in his grasp, owing to their rotten condition, but their removal disclosed a quantity of human remains beneath, packed in shavings, which, like the new coffin, (for it was nothing less) that held them were damp and discoloured. This unexpected and disconcerting revelation brought the workers face to face with the condition that Mr Raine's coffin and the bones it contained should not be tampered with.[27]

Dean Kitchin's memory is subtly different however. He says that " . . . the coffin of 1827 had broken asunder under the pressure of rubbish *over* it."

However, whether or not there was actually "rubbish" on top of the coffin as well as below, it is clear that the container that had been put together by Raine had failed.

The investigators were now faced with a dilemma for which they had not prepared. Canon Fowler's "official" account reads:

> And now came the question how this frail and shabby packing-case, for it was nothing more, could be removed without disturbing its contents. Unless it were taken out, it was impossible to secure the remains of early coffins on which it lay, or properly to examine the

masonry of the grave. An attempt was accordingly made to encase it in new boards with iron bands passed round them, or to protect it in any way that might seem feasible as the work went on. The most skilful and patient efforts of the clerk of the works and his labourers to this end occupied the remainder of this day and some hours of the next, but proved to be unsuccessful. Indeed, the only result was the complete disintegration of the decayed remains of the packing-case, and the unseemly spectacle of human bones, rotten shavings, etc. already referred to.

In these unexpected circumstances it was felt that the most reverent treatment of the human remains would be to effect a careful "translation," with a view to their being finally deposited in the grave in a decent manner; that to adopt this course would enable the bones to be carefully examined, and would make it easy to take out whatever there might be underneath them. A temporary shell or coffin, lined with cotton wool and white linen, was at once prepared, and on 2 March, at about 2 p.m., the work of "translation" began. This continued through the whole of the afternoon, the bones of the principal skeleton, which were mostly in their right places, being arranged by me in their proper order in the temporary coffin, while the many other bones found with these, including the cloven portions of a skull, which we suppose to have been St Oswald's, were laid separately in other receptacles.

Meanwhile the chanting of those same Psalms and Canticles that had so often formed the praises of the holy dead, sounded in our ears as the afternoon service was being sung in the choir, and indeed, to use the words of the Rev. W. Brown, "It was a rather solemn and impressive task, and was carried through very reverently."

The first thing they did was to send for a "competent anatomist" to help them examine the relics. And then they ordered a new coffin. This was to become the eighth such encasement in which Cuthbert had been laid, each of which told its own story: Raine's "frail and shabby packing-case"; the outer coffin he had discovered in 1827 with its lid dished upwards "like a scroll of parchment shrivelled before the fire"; the medieval gilded shrine-cover with its silver bells and "four lively images curious to the beholders"; the eleventh-century ornamental box, decorated with gold and precious stones that was described by Reginald; the hidebound Viking-era travelling chest; the carved Anglo-Saxon coffin-reliquary; all the way back to Abbot Cudda's stone sarcophagus which Cuthbert had with him on Inner Farne and which itself contained the linen cloth given to him by Abbess Verca in which he wanted to be buried.

The new coffin was to be made of oak and to be "rectangular in shape, substantial in structure, and an altogether different thing from the wretched case, which in 1827 Mr Raine dignified with the appellation 'coffin'".[28] A crown (for St Oswald) and a representation of the pectoral cross were to be carved on its lid.

At every point the investigators, and Father Brown in particular, wanted to reassure the Roman Catholic community that the unanticipated disturbance of Cuthbert's remains was done with respect. Tactfully, none of the accounts point out what seems to have been the case: that Raine had actually thrown the bones of other saints back into the grave along with the "broken wood, iron rings, and iron bars". However, there were still some differences between the religions. Both the Anglican university men were keen to emphasise that the skeleton of St Cuthbert was easily distinguishable from the other bones in the grave.

"The bones of the chief body were found arranged loosely in their natural order," says Dean Kitchin, while Canon Fowler quotes the anatomist who had been brought in:

"The bones of the skeleton supposed to be that of Saint Cuthbert were uniformly of a deep brownish tint," he writes, "and, being quite different in appearance, texture, and formation from those of other relics found in the vault, left, by their similarities as well as by their position in the grave, no doubt that they belonged to the same skeleton."

Father Brown's position is different. He was a proponent of a Roman Catholic tradition that, sometime during the reformation, Cuthbert's corpse had been spirited away and hidden in another part of the Cathedral in order to protect it from further desecration, and that a substitute skeleton had been taken from the graveyard, robed and left in its place. Unfortunately, Father Brown's serialised, contemporaneous account of the 1899 opening gives out with the following words, as if he cannot bring himself to make a definitive statement.

> Here, much against my will, I must pause for the present. I have much more to say, especially in reference to the bones, which were disentombed; but this is the 22nd day of June, and the publishing date of the Magazine impends, urging a truce to writing. If God spares me, I hope to have the third and final portion of this article ready for our December issue.[29]

But the third and final instalment never came.

The investigators now had before them a skull, a separated skeleton (with its own skull) and many additional bones. Canon Fowler and Dean Kitchin are willing to attribute these three sets of remains to the sainted King Oswald, St Cuthbert, and to the category "miscellaneous bones".

The skull they identify as that of St Oswald had been hacked about, just as might be expected of a king who died in battle. These are the anatomist's notes.

> A large cut . . . beginning on the left side, extended for about three and one-eighths of an inch on to a much smaller fragment of the left parietal bone for about one inch. The cut was in a downward and forward direction, and indicated a blow from a heavy, sharp

weapon, having been struck by someone on the left side of the victim. On the extreme right of this cut, and at its termination, the inner table of the skull is fractured off to the extent of one and a quarter inch by five-eighths of an inch. With this exception, the cut is perfectly clean through outer and inner tables of the skull, with sharp edges, until the left extremity is reached, when the bone becomes again jagged, as though fractured off by the leverage of the weapon and the blow after it had penetrated to a certain depth. In all probability the anterior part of the skull was shorn off by the blow.

An oblong fragment of the right parietal bone shows on its posterior border a second clean cut wound, but evidently given from the right side, and in a much more vertical direction. It may have been given after the king fell from the effect of the first described and larger wound.

In comparison, the perfectly preserved skull identified as Cuthbert's looks like one that could belong to so dignified a saint, and it is certainly that of a man who was the right age when he died.

It is the skull on which the greatest interest centres. It is one of a mixed type, with no strongly-marked racial characters. Inclining to the dolichocephalic [long-headed] type, it is a well-balanced head, and the face in life probably showed great "character", the nose being a prominent feature. It is in a very perfect state of preservation.

On many parts of the skull, notably the sockets of eyes, roof of mouth, malar bones, etc., adheres [a} membranous structure. Some portions of a silken texture were attached to the back of the skull, which was also a good deal whitened on the top by a limy deposit. The socket of the right eye was loosely filled with a plug, showing traces of a laminated structure, and with some deposit of whitish saline matter on its outer surface. The plug was not chalk or anything of that nature.

Canon Fowler has another explanation. He sees the thing in the right eye-socket as a desiccated eyeball. "I could distinguish not only the exsiccated muscles diverging from a point at the back," he is quoted as saying, "but the circular form of the iris and the rows of the roots of the eyelashes . . . I have no doubt that it was a shrivelled eyeball, including the lids."[30]

Despite their both being medically trained, the anatomist can offer Fowler no support for his idea that one of Cuthbert's eyes had survived. However, the anatomist *is* convinced that the evidence for disease on the skeleton is consistent with the infirmities from which Cuthbert suffered. He writes:

> It is worthy of note that every recorded illness of Saint Cuthbert is connected with a swelling, and that all his troubles were in the region of joints, viz. the acrid tumour of the knee, the "bubo" in the groin, the callosity at the junction of foot and leg, and lastly the ulcer of the foot. This is I think almost diagnostic of tubercular mischief . . .

The difficulty is that there is no evidence for any of these diseases on the skeleton itself. Two of the vertebrae are fused together, and some "ulcerative process" had eaten away at the junction of the breastbone and the right collar bone. The anatomist finds it odd that Bede did not mention this.

> But though we have no direct evidence that St Cuthbert during life suffered from any trouble in these regions, with regard to the disease of the vertebrae, this was of such a character that there need not have been any outward manifestation during life. It is difficult, however, to believe that the extensive disease of the sternum and clavicle should not have given visible evidence during life. Be that as it may, and allowing for the fact that such a sinus as must have resulted would hardly, if known, have been forgotten

by so painstaking an historian as Beda, with his faithful record of other "swellings," it should not be forgotten that there need not have been more external sign that a small sinus, and that the skin over the clavicle quickly ulcerating through, there would be no prolonged accumulation of pus to attract attention. Again, it is possible the disease continued during Saint Cuthbert's anchorite life; and, moreover, it was in such a position which would not entail lameness or temporary loss of the use of any limb . . . Not only that, he could easily attend to it himself without assistance, and he would doubtless, from its very situation, be keenly anxious to hide the sore from the knowledge of others.

But though the signs of disease found on the bones does not demonstrate any known lesion existing in life, there is a very great difficulty in believing that, if a "made up" skeleton were substituted for the genuine Saint Cuthbert at or after the visit of the Commissioners in 1537, one should be chosen from the Cathedral graveyard (as is alleged by the Benedictines) which would agree so closely with the particulars we know relating to Saint Cuthbert.

Essentially, the identification of the skeleton with Cuthbert comes down to five factors. It had the type of long-headed skull the investigators associated with people of the period; it was the right height; it was the right age; it had the right kind of disease (although in the wrong part of the body); and it was in the right place.

There are however some discrepancies between the accounts. Canon Fowler fails to mention that a thigh bone is missing, something that both Dean Kitchin and Father Brown state plainly. This is Dean Kitchin:

When the bones were laid out for us and counted up, before being deposited in the new oaken coffin, it was found that only one important member was missing, one of the thigh bones; this may be the "leg" which was broken up by the goldsmith with his hammer.

Nine years later, in a letter to the local paper, Father Brown finally managed to complete his account of the day:

> I must recall something that occurred on March 2nd, 1899. A careful attempt was being made to raise from the vault the "new coffin" in which Canon Raine had placed the remains found by him on May 17th 1827. The shoddy thing collapsed and the contents, consisting chiefly of his "skeleton of saint Cuthbert" fell out, and were scattered among a mass of bones and broken wood that lay at the bottom of the grave. However, with the least possible delay the vault was cleared and human remains sufficient not only for a skeleton but with about 180 bones to spare, were brought to light. The collection included three lower jaws, about 20 ribs, 35 bones of feet, 26 portions of backbone, seven left shin bones etc in addition to those selected to form a skeleton, which during the following fortnight was pieced together from the abundant material at hand. On the morning of March 17th that skeleton, enclosed in a beautiful new coffin of oak, was consigned to "Saint Cuthbert's Grave, in the Feretory, and there it now lies—*minus*, however a left shin bone (tibia). In this respect it differs from the skeleton found by Canon Raine in 1827, which was complete. If a departure from the original has been made in this particular detail, is it not to be feared that other differences may also have been introduced and actually exist, even to the insertion for foreign bones because they seemed to give token of ailments mentioned by the Venerable Bede? Seven left shin bones were available, one of them certainly belonging to Raine's find. Why were they all discarded as forming part of the new skeleton? Something is wrong with it or with its predecessor of 1827. Which was it? And how much of the 1827 skeleton is contained in the present occupant of the Feretory vault? We require something more satisfactory and certain than it to venerate as Saint Cuthbert's 'mortal frame'."[31]

But there is perhaps one overriding feature that makes it more likely that the identified skeleton is that of St Cuthbert: there is evidence of mummification that Raine had missed or not wanted to see. According to the the anatomist, the bones of the skeleton are sheathed:

> They were in many places covered with a membranous layer, particles of which, being burnt, gave off a marked animal odour. This odour was also observed in the case of a particle taken from a piece of dry, greyish material, which fell through the foramen magnum during the examination of the skull . . .
>
> It is quite possible that the remains existed for a long time in a mummified condition, and the adherence of a membranous covering or layer still discernible on the bones is strong evidence of such a fact.

The 1899 investigators have come as far as they can. They found a few more fragments from the coffin-reliquary as well as other bits and pieces from the shine. They greatly strengthened the "presumption that the almost complete skeleton is that of Saint Cuthbert" and they have "all but positively" identified the skull of St Oswald. Perhaps more importantly, they have straightened out the mess left by Raine, and Cuthbert's long-venerated relics are to be "entombed under decent and honourable conditions of sepulture."

> On Friday, March 17th, the whole of the bones, having been duly deposited in the new coffin, were restored to the grave. In the upper part of the coffin were placed the bones forming the skeleton supposed to be Saint Cuthbert's, and with these, as of old, the cloven skull of Saint Oswald. The other relics were laid under the horizontal partition above mentioned. Within the coffin was placed a bottle containing a Churchman's Almanac for 1899, and a properly attested account of the recent investigation.

The coffin was carried through the cloister and the church, the dean and the sacrist walking before it in surplices and conducting a short service by the grave. The sacred relics were once more laid to rest, and the two grave covers, with the intermediate gravel and the floor stones that had been taken up, were replaced exactly as before.

It is still there.

Epilogue

20 March 687

The mystery of Cuthbert's incorrupt corpse is not, after all this, very mysterious. If you condense the accounts of the six openings to a brutalist minimum, the sequence of decay is unremarkable, if admittedly extended. In 689, someone wrapped or bandaged Cuthbert's emaciated body; 698, the corpse is found to be mummified; 934, the mummy's limbs can be articulated; 1104, the mummy's limbs can still be articulated but it collapses in the middle when lifted (in his public demonstration the Abbot of Séez only raises the corpse to a sitting position); 1539, the mummy still has some integrity when laid in the coffin (although exposure to the air between 1539–42 perhaps caused massive deterioration); 1827, it is now a complete skeleton, its skull detachable; 1899, all that is left is skull and miscellaneous bones.

But there are other mysteries to occupy the mind. One of the strangest is the existence of the golden-garnet cross. Undoubtedly Anglo-Saxon, it dates like Cuthbert from the very earliest years of Christianity in the land that would become England. But it is also a strange thing to find on the body of a hermit. That Cuthbert was a committed ascetic is attested by his biographers, and it seems reasonable that his extreme commitment to deprivation on Inner Farne is demonstrated by the part it played in preparing his body for preservation. We also know from the accounts of his time as prior and bishop that he maintained his hermetical values in office. And we know what Aelfflaed said to him on Coquet island: "thou rejectest the glory of the world, although it is offered thee". So a rich jewel is an odd thing to find on his emaciated body.

It is intriguing too that what we know of the provenance of three of the other four pectoral crosses that have been found from this period is that they are associated with the burial of high-status women (the fourth is unknown). And, as much as he rejected the glory of the world, Cuthbert was certainly often recorded as being in the company of high-status women.

Thirdly, there is the strangeness of its disappearance from the record for 1100 years. It is a sumptuous jewel, associated with one of the most attested corpses in history, yet not one of the seven accounts of the openings of the coffin mentions the cross until Raine discovered it in 1827.

Bede and Cuthbert's anonymous biographer do not mention it. There is no community memory of it recorded through the Viking period. Symeon and his fellow monks fail to record seeing it in 1104. It even evades the very men who were employed to rifle through venerated human detritus to find precious metals and jewels on behalf of Henry VIII. Which creates another mystery.

Why did Leigh, Henley and Blytham not find it? Indeed, why did they not see the silver altar? Because, no matter how small and concealed the cross, the silver altar was not a thing that would have been easy to miss in an under-sized coffin. One explanation is that, having already found a jewel sufficient to redeem a prince, Leigh, Henley and Blytham were happy to call it a day; although Henley's repeated instruction to cast down the bones does not sound like that of someone knocking off for the afternoon. Another possibility is that the missing jewel was never missing: it was well known but never recorded, and was hidden from the three officials along with the altar and only added to the coffin when the corpse was finally lowered into its grave in 1542. This occurred despite the very real danger of torture and death: the Abbot of Glastonbury had just been hung, drawn and quartered for hiding valuables in this way. Concealment is strengthened as an explanation because, in 2011, what looks like a tiny copy of the cross was found in the River Wear.

A pilgrim's souvenir cast in pewter, the find has been dated to the early fifteenth century but is currently the only one we know about. If confirmed, it is a discovery that could only mean the cross was outside the coffin during some of the medieval period.[32]

Yet this would create more mystery. Perhaps the cross was like the Lindisfarne Gospels, simply another treasure from the period, and Cuthbert was not associated with it until both were finally consigned to the same grave in 1542. Perhaps the cross was found on the corpse or placed on it during unrecorded openings of the coffin: a possibility that might give credence to Father Brown's support for the theory that the skeleton found by Raine was a decoy and that the real corpse of St Cuthbert is hidden elsewhere in the Cathedral. Or perhaps the cross was indeed placed on the corpse in 687 or 698 but then found by the Normans in 1104 . This would account for the odd emphasis Reginald places on all the probing and touching by "inquisitive hands" while also explaining his hint that the investigators had "learnt every secret concerning him".

Or perhaps the traditional explanation is right after all and it was always there, placed so far beneath the wrappings that it remained undetected for over a thousand years. As Raine said, it was "found deeply buried among the remains of the robes which were nearest to the breast of the Saint". We may never know.

But it is a strange combination of circumstances: a sumptuous jewel on a hermit's body; one that was overlooked by all the chroniclers for over a millennium; an ornament associated with aristocratic women; its curving arms patterned like the metalwork at Whitby Abbey, Aelfflaed's home.

We are never likely to know how the cross came to be on Cuthbert's corpse. But, in 1383, almost 700 years after his death, a winding sheet and vestment from that first burial were still preserved in Durham Cathedral. The sheet had a "double texture", noted the shrine keeper, adding that it was the one which had "enveloped the body of Saint Cuthbert in his grave". It is assumed the attribution that follows must be an error for Abbess Verca, who provided the cloth, but the list is very certain. It says, "Aelfflaed the Abbess had wrapped him up in it". [33]

Bibliography

William M. Aird, *St Cuthbert and the Normans: The Church of Durham, 1071-1153* (Boydell Press, 1998).

ANONYMOUS (George Bates), *The Rites of Durham, being a description or brief declaration of all the ancient monuments, rites, & customs belonging or being within the monastical church of Durham before the suppression* (Surtees Society, 1903).

C.F. Battiscombe, ed., *The Relics of Saint Cuthbert: Studies by Various Authors* (Oxford University Press, 1956).

Gerald Bonner, David Rollason and Clare Stancliffe, eds., *St Cuthbert, His Cult and His Community to AD 1200* (Boydell Press, 1989).

Diana Boyson, *The Coffins of Saint Cuthbert* (Durham PhD Thesis, 1974).

Peter Brown, *The Cult of the Saints: Its Rise and Function in Latin Christianity* (University of Chicago Press, 1981).

William Brown, "Saint Cuthbert's Grave and Coffin", *The Ushaw Magazine 9* (1899).

William Brown, "Saint Cuthbert's Remains", *The Ushaw Magazine 19* (1909).

Bertram Colgrave, *Two Lives of Saint Cuthbert: a life by an anonymous monk of Lindisfarne and Bede's prose life* (Cambridge University Press, 1940).

Robert Colls, *Northumbria: History and Identity 547–2000* (The History Press, 2007).

J.M. Cronyn and C.V. Horie, *Saint Cuthbert's Coffin* (Durham Cathedral, 1985).

C. Eyre, *The History of Saint Cuthbert* (London, 1887).

J.T. Fowler, "On an Examination of the Grave of Saint Cuthbert", *Archaeologia 57* (1900).

John Allen Giles, *The Biographical Writing and Letters of Venerable Bede* (Bohn, 1845).

George William Kitchin, "The Contents of Saint Cuthbert's Shrine", *The Victoria History of the Counties of England: Durham* (Archibald Constable & Co., 1905).

John Lingard, *Remarks on the "Saint Cuthbert" of the Rev. James Raine, M.A.* (Newcastle, 1828).

Norman Emery, "The Remains and Relics of Saint Cuthbert", *Durham Cathedral Archaeology Report 23* (2004).

Dominic Marner, *St. Cuthbert: His Life and Cult in Medieval Durham* (British Library, 2000).

Geoffrey Moorhouse, *The Last Office: 1539 and the Dissolution of a Monastery* (Phoenix, 2009).

C. Peers and C.A. Ralegh Radford, "The Saxon Monastery at Whitby", *Archaeologia 89* (1943).

James Raine, *Saint Cuthbert: with an account of the state in which his remains were found upon the opening of his tomb in Durham Cathedral, in the year MDCCCXXVII* (Geoffrey Andrews, 1828).

D.W. Rollason, ed., *Cuthbert: Saint and Patron* (Dean and Chapter of Durham, 1987).

David Rollason (ed.), *Symeon of Durham: Libellus de Exordio atque Procursu istius, hoc est Dunhelmensis, Ecclesie* (Clarendon Press, 2000).

David Rollason, Margaret Harvey and Michael Prestwich (eds.), *Anglo-Norman Durham 1093–1193* (Boydell Press, 1994).

David Rollason and Michael Prestwich (eds.), *The Battle of Neville's Cross* (Shaun Tyas, 1998).

Ted Johnson South, *Historia De Sancto Cuthberti: A History of Saint Cuthbert and a Record of his Patrimony* (D.S. Brewer, 2001).

J.F. Webb, *The Age of Bede* (Penguin, 1988).

Endnotes

1   All translations of Bede are from John Allen Giles, *The Biographical Writing and Letters of Venerable Bede* (London, 1845).

2   All translations of the anonymous biographer are from Bertram Colgrave, *Two Lives of Saint Cuthbert* (Cambridge, 1940).

3   Elizabeth Coatsworth, "The Pectoral Cross and Portable Altar from the Tomb of Saint Cuthbert", in Gerald Bonner, David Rollason and Clare Stancliffe (eds.), *St Cuthbert, His Cult and His Community to AD 1200* (Boydell Press, 1989).

4   R.L.S. Bruce-Mitford, "The Pectoral Cross", in C.F. Battiscombe (ed.), *The Relics of Saint Cuthbert* (Oxford University Press, 1956), p. 324.

5   Translation: Benjamin Thorpe, *The Anglo-Saxon Chronicle* (Longman, Green, Longman and Roberts, 1861), p. 48.

6   Translation: Joseph Stevenson, "The Historical Works of Simeon of Durham", *The Church Historians of England 3* (Seeleys, 1855), p. 457.

7   Translation: Ted Johnson South, *Historia De Sancto Cuthberti* (D.S. Brewer, 2001), pp. 65–7.

8   David Rollason (ed.), *Symeon of Durham* (Clarendon Press, 2000).

9   Translation: James Raine, *Saint Cuthbert* (Geoffrey Andrews, 1828), p. 93.

10 Both translations of Reginald and the anonymous monk are from ibid., pp. 75–93.

11 Descriptions of the shrine: ANONYMOUS [George Bates], *The Rites of Durham* (Surtees Society, 1803), pp. 3–5.

12 Quoted in Geoffrey Moorhouse, *The Last Office* (Phoenix, 2009).

13 Quoted in ibid., p. 118.

14 Quoted in ibid., p. 119.

15 ANONYMOUS [George Bates], *The Rites of Durham* (Surtees Society, 1903), pp. 85–6.

16 C. Eyre, *The History of Saint Cuthbert* (London, 1887), pp. 184–5.

17 James Raine, *Saint Cuthbert* (Geoffrey Andrews, 1828), pp. 179–80.

18 John Lingard, *Remarks on the "Saint Cuthbert" of the Rev. James Raine, M.A.* (Newcastle, 1828), pp. 1–2.

19 James Raine, *Saint Cuthbert* (Geoffrey Andrews, 1828), pp. 180–216.

20 Richard Bailey, "Saint Cuthbert's Relics: Some Neglected Evidence", in Gerald Bonner, David Rollason and Clare Stancliffe, eds., *St Cuthbert, His Cult and His Community to AD 1200* (Boydell Press, 1989), p. 232.

21 Quoted in ibid., p. 233.

22 Quoted in ibid., pp. 233–4.

23 Quoted in ibid., p. 231.

24 J.T. Fowler, "On an Examination of the Grave of Saint Cuthbert", *Archaeologia* 57 (1900).

25 George William Kitchin, "The Contents of Saint Cuthbert's Shrine", *The Victoria History of the Counties of England: Durham* (Archibald Constable & Co., 1905).

26 William Brown, "Saint Cuthbert's Grave and Coffin", *The Ushaw Magazine 9* (1899), p. 125.

27 Ibid., pp. 126–7.

28 Ibid., p. 132.

29 Ibid., p. 132.

30 Quoted in George William Kitchin, "The Contents of Saint Cuthbert's Shrine", *The Victoria History of the Counties of England: Durham* (Archibald Constable & Co., 1905), pp. 232–3.

31 William Brown, "Saint Cuthbert's Remains", *The Ushaw Magazine 19* (1909), pp. 28–9.

32 Found by Gary Bankhead (Portable Antiquities Scheme reference: PUBLIC-9CD231; other reference: Bankhead 2301).

33 Quoted in James Raine, *Saint Cuthbert* (Geoffrey Andrews, 1828), p. 128.

Lightning Source UK Ltd.
Milton Keynes UK
UKHW020653150123
415356UK00017B/92